ACCESS IN THE INFORMATION AGE:
COMMUNITY COLLEGES
BRIDGING THE DIGITAL DIVIDE

Edited by

Gerardo E. de los Santos
Alfredo G. de los Santos Jr.
Mark David Milliron

League for Innovation in the Community College

elementk

Published with support from Element K.
For more information, see page 129.
www.elementk.com

ISBN 1-931300-24-0

TABLE OF CONTENTS

ACKNOWLEDGMENTS 7

INTRODUCTION 9

CHAPTER 1 17
Access in the Information Age: Community Colleges Bridging the Digital Divide
*Gerardo E. de los Santos, Vice President for Alliance Services, League for Innovation in the Community College, CA; **Alfredo G. de los Santos Jr.**, Research Professor, Arizona State University, Main, Senior League Fellow, League for Innovation in the Community College, AZ, **Mark David Milliron**, President and Chief Executive Officer, League for Innovation in the Community College, CA*

CHAPTER 2 23
A Divide at Our Door: A Review of Trend Literature Related to the Digital Divide
***Alfredo G. de los Santos Jr.**, Research Professor, Arizona State University, Main, Senior League Fellow, League for Innovation in the Community College, AZ*

CHAPTER 3 35
Technology-Based Occupational Education Programs: Short-Term Training With Lasting Advantages
***Stella Perez**, Director, League Online, League for Innovation in the Community College, CA*

CHAPTER 4 43
Bridging the Digital Divide: Supporting the Learning Journey of College Faculty and Staff
***Ruth Mclean**, Associate Dean, Centre for Learner Support, Humber College of Applied Arts and Technology, Toronto*

CHAPTER 5 53
Maricopa's Ocotillo: Connectivity for Curriculum, Technology, and Pedagogy
Alfredo G. de los Santos Jr., Research Professor, Arizona State University Main and Senior League Fellow, League for Innovation, AZ; Naomi O. Story, Director, Center for Teaching and Learning, Maricopa Community Colleges, AZ

CHAPTER 6 61
Developing a Technology Plan to Continuously Support and Enhance Effectiveness in Teaching and Learning
Leonardo de la Garza, *Chancellor, Tarrant County College District, TX*

CHAPTER 7 69
An Urban Two-Year Campus Strives to Narrow the Digital Divide Through Access and Partnerships
Alex B. Johnson, Campus President; Patricia Mintz, Dean, Business and Technology; Paul Abiola, Manager, Technology Learning Center; and Erika Bell, Staff Assistant, Metropolitan Campus, Cuyahoga Community College, OH

CHAPTER 8 77
Preparing K-12 Teachers in the Use of Technology: Community Colleges Address the Digital Divide
Edward J. Leach, Vice President, Technology Programs, League for Innovation in the Community College, CA

CHAPTER 9 85
A Strategy of Scale: Foundations of Information Technology Literacy and Support Structures to Bridge the Digital Divide
Maryann Fraboni, *Vice President, Strategic Initiatives;* **Susan Muha**, *Executive Vice President, Workforce and Economic Development, Cuyahoga Community College, OH*

CHAPTER 10 95
Digital Divide: A New Term for an Old Problem
Robert E. Griffin, Vice President, Student Services, De Anza College, CA

CHAPTER 11 103
A Solution for Digitally Disenfranchised Students
Kimball B. **Kendall**, *Director, Center for Academic Technologies;* **Pat Smittle**, *Associate, Vice President;* **Patricia Grunder**, *Vice President, Santa Fe Community College, FL*

CHAPTER 12 113
Increasing Numbers, Increasing Needs: Where Do We Go From Here?
Gerardo E. de los Santos, Vice President for Alliance Services, League for Innovation in the Community College, CA; **Alfredo G. de los Santos Jr.**, *Research Professor, Arizona State University Main and Senior League Fellow, League for Innovation in the Community College AZ;* **Mark David Milliron**, *President and Chief Operating Officer, League for Innovation in the Community College, CA*

ACKNOWLEDGMENTS

This book is the result of many dedicated educators and colleagues who are committed to providing educational opportunities and information access for all students. Mil gracias (a thousand thanks) to the contributing authors who selflessly shared their Digital Divide experiences and successes in the chapters that follow–without their generous contributions, this book would not have been possible.

Special thanks to Amado M. Peña, Jr., internationally renowned Southwestern artist and Laredo Community College Distinguished Graduate, for creating and donating the cover art for this book. Pena's commitment and support of community colleges is highly regarded and we are delighted and honored that he is partnering with the League on this important project.

And, muchisimas gracias (very special thanks) and warm appreciation to our colleagues at the League who reviewed the manuscript, Cindy L. Miles, Cynthia Wilson, Nancy Italia, and Edward J. Leach. At the League, we proudly tout that our accomplishments are team efforts–the reviewing of this book was clearly such an effort. To that end, we also acknowledge and thank the League support staff who daily assist our efforts to ensure quality in everything we do.

INTRODUCTION

Gerardo E. de los Santos, Alfredo G. de los Santos Jr.,
Mark David Milliron

With Information Age advancements in technology, new and exciting approaches to working, playing, and learning are commonplace. Today we have the ability to access and use information in unprecedented ways, and our access options are changing and growing daily. The rate of change in communications and technology hardware, software, and training is so staggering that it is causing a revolutionary response in the workplace, at home, and in education. In the new global economy, driven by information technology, the majority of jobs created in the workforce require technological literacy skills; increasing numbers of basic services—banking, shopping, and travel planning, for example—and information are available on the Web, also requiring technology skills. Traditional methods for delivering instruction are changing and expanding dramatically, requiring technology skills of both instructors and students.

The exciting and beneficial changes of this technological revolution have extended a divide that has long been the challenge and opportunity for community college educators. The Digital Divide in which these technological benefits are less accessible to a growing number of traditionally underrepresented populations is a technological extension of the divide that has long existed between traditionally underrepresented populations and the majority population. The extension and focus of the Digital Divide encompasses communications, technology, and training access.

Historically, community colleges welcome and serve underrepresented populations that have been separated from any number of different divides. Technology challenges community college educators with another complex divide. For community colleges to help address the challenges of the Digital Divide, they must develop innovative, collaborative, and assertive approaches to serving a growing number of digitally distant, traditionally underrepresented students.

Access in the Information Age: Community Colleges Bridging the Digital Divide is one of many League efforts aimed at inspiring community college educators to take the strategic steps that will help provide the necessary information technology access and skill sets for a growing number of underserved and economically challenged populations. This publication is a call for community college educators to move beyond definition and dialogue about the Digital Divide and take action. Specifically, this volume (1) defines and describes the Digital Divide in the community college context; (2) reviews the literature; and (3) describes model programs and successful strategies based on key recommendations. Each chapter provides a strategy for carrying out one of the eight recommendations issued in the League's February 2000 *Leadership Abstract* by Alfredo G. de los Santos Jr. and Gerardo E. de los Santos, "Community Colleges Bridging the Digital Divide."

Chapter Overviews and Recommendations

In the chapters that follow, the contributors to this volume describe model programs and successful strategies for carrying out the eight recommendations. These recommendations exemplify how some of the most innovative community colleges in the world are building bridges across the Digital Divide. Because the issues central to the Digital Divide are far reaching and often involve broad strategies, the chapters range from institutional to programmatic strategies and models.

CHAPTER 1
Access in the Information Age: Community Colleges Bridging the Digital Divide

Community colleges play a critical role in helping address the multiple and complex implications of the Digital Divide. This chapter describes the Digital Divide in the community college context, defines technological literary and change savvy as they pertain to the new economy, and shares eight recommendations that serve to guide community college educators dedicated to closing the gap between the information haves and have-nots.

Gerardo E. de los Santos, Vice President for Alliance Services, League for Innovation in the Community College, CA; Alfredo G. de los Santos Jr., Research Professor, Arizona State University, Main and Senior League Fellow, League for Innovation in the Community College, AZ;

Mark David Milliron, President and Chief Operating Officer, League for Innovation in the Community College, CA

CHAPTER 2
A Divide at Our Door: A Review of Trend Literature Related to the Digital Divide

Multiple sources from various segments of society, education, business, and government clearly recognize information access disparities in American society and around the world. This chapter explores the state of information technology access across income, racial and ethnic, age, region, gender, and educational lines. In addition, a profile of community college students is related to information technology access and future college enrollments.

Alfredo G. de los Santos Jr., Research Professor, Arizona State University, Main, Senior League Fellow, League for Innovation in the Community College, AZ

CHAPTER 3
Technology-Based Occupational Education Programs: Short-Term Training With Lasting Advantages

This chapter explores the recommendation that *community colleges should strengthen their occupational and other short-cycle offerings to continue to prepare the growing number of information technology workers needed in the new economy.* Through creative practice and unconventional theory, two progressive community colleges offer new models for training, developing, and preparing a range of students for success in today's information-based society.

Stella Perez, Director, League Online, League for Innovation in the Community College, AZ

CHAPTER 4
Bridging the Digital Divide: Supporting the Learning Journey of College Faculty and Staff

With astounding advancements in information technology challenging traditional approaches to information access and instructional delivery, community college instruction is transforming in new and exciting ways. This chapter explores the recommendation that *community colleges should provide opportunities for all members of the faculty and staff to use computers, the Internet, and other emerging technologies.* This chapter describes the development and implementation of Humber College's one-stop instructional support resource centre, known as the Studio.

Ruth Mclean, Associate Dean, Centre for Learner Support, Humber College of Applied Arts and Technology

CHAPTER 5
Maricopa's Ocotillo: Connectivity for Curriculum, Technology, and Pedagogy

This chapter is based on the recommendation that *community colleges should review the curriculum and pedagogies used in the classroom to ensure that all students develop technology literacy and the ability to adapt quickly to change* and the authors relate how the Maricopa Community College District (MCCD) is bridging the Digital Divide through its development of a faculty-driven organizational structure, Ocotillo, that facilitates collaborative decision making and shared responsibility among faculty, staff, and administrators to solve complex learning issues with and about technology. This organizational structure helps MCCD educators better serve digitally disenfranchised students by systemically improving curriculum and pedagogies designed to ensure that all students develop technology literacy.

Alfredo G. de los Santos Jr., Research Professor, Arizona State University, Main and Senior League Fellow, League for Innovation in the Community College, AZ; Naomi O. Story, Director, Center for Teaching and Learning, Maricopa Community College District, AZ

CHAPTER 6
Developing a Technology Plan to Continuously Support and Enhance Effectiveness in Teaching and Learning

The following chapter is based on the recommendation that *community colleges should develop strategic plans to enhance and continuously improve the use of technology in learning and teaching processes.* Specifically, this chapter represents the systemic efforts of one institution toward laying a strong, strategic foundation to address the technology needs of its staff and students and, ultimately, to extend the opportunities of the Digital Age to all members of its community.

Leonardo de la Garza, Chancellor, Tarrant County College District, TX

CHAPTER 7
An Urban Two-Year Campus Strives to Narrow the Digital Divide Through Access and Partnerships

Cuyahoga Community College (CCC) is committed to technology access to enable residents of Greater Cleveland to acquire the technical skills needed for success in their educational and professional pursuits. This chapter is based on the recommendation that *community colleges should create venues, on their own or with partners, where all students can access computers and the Internet on and off campus* and describes how CCC has successfully created multiple IT access venues for students.

Alex B. Johnson, Campus President; Patricia Mintz, Dean, Business and Technology; Paul Abiola, Manager, Technology Learning Center; and Erika Bell, Staff Assistant, Metropolitan Campus, Cuyahoga Community College

CHAPTER 8
Preparing K-12 Teachers in the Use of Technology: Community Colleges Address the Digital Divide

The glaring disparities outlined in Chapter One create new challenges for educational decision makers. In their *Leadership Abstract,* "Community Colleges Bridging the Digital Divide," de los Santos Jr. and de los Santos call for community colleges *to work with their local K-12 school systems to facilitate the professional development of teachers in the use of technology in teaching and learning processes, particularly in those communities with majority minority populations.* The goal is to look beyond the simplified solution of providing student access to technology and begin adequately training teachers who directly influence and prepare students from low economic communities and communities of color for opportunities in the digital economy.

Edward J. Leach, Vice President, Technology Programs, League for Innovation in the Community College, CA

CHAPTER 9
A Strategy of Scale: Foundations of Information Technology Literacy and Support Structures to Bridge the Digital Divide

Bridging the Digital Divide requires more than hardware, software, and technology training; it requires strategic partnering. To this end, this chapter explores the recommendation that *community colleges should seek relationships with technology partners in their local business communities who will directly and indirectly benefit from technologically literate employee prospects.* This chapter describes the efforts of Cuyahoga Community College to development strategic partnerships with employers in their local business community, as well as package IT skills with job-related soft skills.

Maryann Fraboni, *Vice President, Strategic Initiatives;* **Susan Muha**, *Executive Vice President, Workforce and Economic Development, Cuyahoga Community College, OH*

CHAPTER 10
Digital Divide: A New Term for an Old Problem

This chapter describes De Anza College's efforts to initiate dialogue among faculty, staff, students, and administrators about the role and place of historically underrepresented students, particularly African Americans, in the Digital Age. Based on the recommendation that *community colleges should facilitate explorations of how the issues of growing minority enrollments, limited access to technology, and increasing requirements for technology and change savvy will likely impact them in the future,* this chapter captures an honest, meaningful campus discussion regarding Digital Divide issues and points to how such dialogue can clarify the issues to help institutions develop strategic intentions that move from talk to action.

Robert E. Griffin, Vice President, Student Services, De Anza College, CA

CHAPTER 11
A Solution for Digitally Disenfranchised Students

With more digitally disadvantaged students entering our open doors, community college educators are challenged to assess and address students' various levels of technology literacy. This chapter is based on the recommendation that *community colleges should review curriculum and pedagogies used in the classroom to ensure that all students develop technology literacy and the ability to adapt quickly to change.* Specifically, this chapter describes how Santa Fe Community College developed the Business Information Technology Career Assistance Program, a year-long support program designed to help improve technology skills for historically underrepresented students.

Kimball B. Kendall, *Director, Center for Academic Technologies;* ***Pat Smittle,*** *Associate, Vice President;* ***Patricia Grunder,*** *Vice President, Santa Fe Community College*

CHAPTER 12
Increasing Numbers, Increasing Needs: Where Do We Go From Here?

This concluding chapter describes the overlap between many community college students and members of our society who have limited access to information technology. In addition, this chapter provides community college leaders a five-part framework for addressing Digital Divide issues as they relate to helping increase information technology access and training for their students and community. Finally, a more systemic framework based on the concept of Learner Relationship Management is proposed, a framework that can catalyze conversations about outfitting community colleges to create more lasting relationships with those needing to cross the bridge over the Digital Divide.

Gerardo E. de los Santos, *Vice President for Alliance Services, League for Innovation in the Community College, CA;* ***Alfredo G. de los Santos Jr.,*** *Research Professor, Arizona State University, Main and Senior League Fellow, League for Innovation in the Community College, AZ;* ***Mark David Milliron,*** *President and Chief Operating Officer, League for Innovation in the Community College, CA*

CHAPTER 1

ACCESS IN THE INFORMATION AGE: COMMUNITY COLLEGES BRIDGING THE DIGITAL DIVIDE

Gerardo E. de los Santos, Alfredo G. de los Santos Jr., Mark David Milliron

The lack of technology access and skills puts disadvantaged members of our society increasingly at risk of becoming disenfranchised spectators of a digital world that is passing them by bit by bit.

– Mark David Milliron and Cindy L. Miles (2000)

Advances in information technology continue to astound us. As a society, we have unparalleled access to information, communication capacities that look and feel like science fiction, and tools for business productivity that are raising Wall Street numbers to all-time highs. Breakthroughs in hardware, software, and communication technologies are also driving change at disconcerting speeds. These rapidly evolving opportunities and challenges mark our place in the Digital Age, where almost all new jobs require some level of information technology skill and the ability to adapt to rapid change. However, these advances also point to our place in the Digital Divide, where this technology is increasingly realized on only one side of the racial ravine. Data from multiple sources make it clear: the Digital Age is disproportionately distant from minority, economically challenged, and disabled populations, and the distance across the divide is increasing.

These trends inspire us–community college educators–to become bridge builders. But, to build effective bridges, we must design three key imperatives into our plans. First, we must prepare for the waves of minority and economically challenged students with significant linguistic and cultural differences who are knocking at our open door. In addition to addressing other issues that have challenged these cohorts in the past, we now must grapple with the significant lack of access to technology with which they come to us. Finally, we must do more than provide these students with access to technology. We also must ensure that they develop a technology base that allows them to use technology well and that they acquire the ability to recognize and adapt to the pace of change in the Digital Age.

Knocking on the Open Door

With a tradition of open door admissions, low tuition, flexible programming, customized student services, and quality learning opportunities, community colleges continue to be the pathway to higher education for about half of all minority undergraduates. Furthermore, community colleges have historically served a high percentage of society's have-nots. Specifically, 55 percent of Hispanic and Native American Indian and 46 percent of African-American undergraduates are enrolled in community colleges (NTIA, 1999).

Based on U.S. Census Bureau data, by the year 2015, minority enrollments in community colleges are projected to increase by approximately 12 percent, while the White student population will decrease by approximately 8 percent. These shifts in student demographics, coupled with the rapid rate of advancement in information technology, send a clear message to community college leaders: the majority of digitally disenfranchised students will be knocking on the community college's open door.

As community colleges continue their commitment to provide educational access to all students–the "at-risk," the "have nots," the high school graduates, the returning adult learner, and the growing number of GED recipients–they must take an aggressive stance in finding quality ways to teach and reach our diverse student population. This mandate is reinforced by the growing number of our students who have a significantly low level of access to information technology.

Technology Access

Computers and the Web have created an explosion of learning opportunities for students at every level, but these digitally-driven opportunities are not being realized by all students. Access to computers and the Internet varies greatly among socioeconomic, racial, and ethnic groups. Alarmingly, a significant number of low-income and minority students are unable to access computers and the Web at home or in school, and the gap continues to widen. Although more than half of all White households have computers and Internet access, less than a quarter of African-American and Hispanic families have computers at home and less than ten percent of these families have home access to the Internet (NTIA, 1999).

Not surprisingly, access to technology in the home is directly related to family income. A National Telecommunications and Information Administration report (2000) indicates that over 75 percent of households with incomes over $75,000 have at least one computer, compared to less than 32 percent of households with incomes between $25,000 and $35,000. The poorer families have significantly less access to this technology.

For children who are considered the haves in the Digital Age, familiarity with the use of computers and the Internet often begins before elementary school. Nonetheless, as more and more learning opportunities via computers and the Web are being introduced and embraced in elementary, middle, and secondary schools, these K-12 institutions are viewed as the first gateway to information literacy for today's youth.

Unfortunately, elementary, middle, and secondary students in schools that serve primarily minority and low-income populations are not benefiting from the use of classroom computers to the same extent as students who attend largely White schools. A 1999 study from The College Board reports, "there is evidence that students with the greatest need get the least access." This finding is corroborated by a recent Educational Testing Service report indicating that schools with the highest concentrations of low-income and minority students have the highest ratio of students to computers, resulting in fewer computer literacy learning opportunities.

Technology and Change Savvy

As we begin the third millennium, computer literacy has become a prerequisite for success in today's workforce. Moreover, the workplace is replete with fundamental and structural changes that challenge participants to adapt more flexibly than ever before. Lester C. Thurow, Dean of the School of Business at Harvard University (1999), argues that the new economy is global, features relentless competition, and offers no such thing as a smooth ride. In this new economy, knowledge builds wealth, and the most important resource is people. Without adequate technology literacy however, this great resource—people—will fail to reach its highest potential.

Technology is a given in the new economy, and how a corporation uses technology will determine its ability to succeed. The new economy may include low-tech companies, but they will not be competitive for long. Even small service businesses such as dry cleaners, hair salons, and car washes are adopting technology to manage customer relationships and maintain a competitive edge. Ultimately, success in the workforce of the new economy will be measured by each person's ability to use technology effectively and efficiently.

This means that simple technology literacy must give way to a focus on comfort with the underpinnings of technology so solid that it allows our students to keep pace with change. More importantly, our students must be able to evaluate critically the mass of information at their fingertips, communicate effectively with their coworkers and customers, and adapt comfortably to an increasingly global economy. In short, they must become *technology and change savvy* at levels heretofore unrealized by many community college educational programs.

Conclusion

Listen to the knock at the open door, consider the needs for technology access, and build into programs and services an emphasis on technology and change savvy as we enter the first phase of bridge building. The chapters that follow will help community college educators aggressively enter this phase and look to a future where all students have access to the opportunities and an understanding of the challenges related to the emerging digital democracy in which we live.

REFERENCES

Carnavale, A. P., & Fry, R. A. (2000). *Crossing the Great Divide: Can We Achieve Equity When Generation Y Goes to College?* Princeton, NJ: Educational Testing Service.

Coley, R. J. (2000). *The American Community College Turns 100: A Look at Its Students, Programs, and Perspectives.* Princeton, NJ: Educational Testing Service.

Gladieux, L. E. & Watson, S. S. (1999). *The Virtual University and Educational Opportunity: Issues of Equity and Access for the Next Generation.* New York: College Board Publications.

National Telecommunications and Information Administration (NTIA). (1999). *Falling Through the Net: Defining the Digital Divide. A Report on the Telecommunications and Information Technology Gap in America.* Washington, DC: U.S. Department of Commerce.

Phillippe, K. A., & Valiga. M. J. (2000). *Faces of the Future: A Portrait of America's Community College Students.* Washington, DC: American Association of Community Colleges.

Phillippe, K. A. (Ed.). (2000). *National Profile of Community Colleges: Trends and Statistics* (3rd ed.). Washington, DC: American Association of Community Colleges.

Thurow, L. C. (1999, June). Building Wealth. *The Atlantic Monthly.*

Western Interstate Commission for Higher Education & The College Board (1998). *Knocking at the College Door.* Boulder, CO: WICHE Publications.

CHAPTER 2

A DIVIDE AT OUR DOOR:
A REVIEW OF TREND LITERATURE
RELATED TO THE DIGITAL DIVIDE

Alfredo G. de los Santos Jr.

Introduction

In an age of instant communications, unprecedented economic growth and prosperity, and unparalleled access to information—all driven by rapid and continuous breakthroughs in information technologies— recent reports clearly show that the United States has a growing Digital Divide, a huge gap between those who have access to these new technologies and those who do not. And the gap is increasing.

While the Digital Divide impacts racial and ethnic groups disproportionately, the level of access is also related to income, education, age, household type, and geography. These levels of access can be described in terms of two major Digital Divide issues: (1) the percent of U.S. homes with a computer and (2) the percent of U.S. families using the Internet at home.

In whatever terms described, however, when we discuss the Digital Divide with educational and political leaders, they seem incredulous. Often, the first reaction is to question whether the Digital Divide truly exists and whether the associated access needs are as severe as those described in the literature and by the media. If the Digital Divide does exist, the second reaction is to question whether it is really a racial or ethnic issue. Detailed information from the most recently available sources can be used to define the question as specifically as possible.

With a detailed definition of the Digital Divide, the community college student profile can be examined in the context of that divide. Further examination focuses on the projected increase in the number of high school graduates and college enrollees, indicating a diversity in higher education never before seen in this country. To define the Digital Divide, an examination of several factors in technology use is required. The National Telecommunications and Information Administration (NTIA) provides revealing statistics on U.S. households with a computer and U.S. households using the Internet.

U.S. Households With a Computer

The percentage of U.S. households with a computer has increased from less than one quarter in 1994 to more than 42 percent in 1998. A slightly higher percentage of households in urban areas had computers at home (42.9 percent) than did rural families (39.9 percent) or families living in the center city (38.5 percent) (NTIA, 1999).

By Income
More than three-fourths of families with annual income of $75,000 or more have a computer at home, whether they live in urban or rural areas or in the center city. Approximately one-half of families whose income is between $35,000 and $49,999 have a computer at home (NTIA, 1999).

Less than one-fourth of families with income of less than $25,000 have a computer at home. In addition, less than 20 percent of families with income of less than $15,000 have computers at home. Around 10 percent of rural families with low income have computers at home, while urban families with incomes of $75,000 or higher are more than nine times more likely to have a computer at home than rural households at the lowest income levels. (NTIA, 1999)

By Race or Ethnic Group
The gap in households with computers between racial and ethnic groups is significant and growing. More than one-half of Asian/Pacific Islander non-Hispanic households (55 percent) and almost half (46.6 percent) of White non-Hispanic households had a computer in 1998 (NTIA, 1999).

Only a fourth of Hispanic households and less than a fourth (23.2 percent) of Black non-Hispanic households had a computer in 1998. The lowest percentage of households with a computer at home were Black non-Hispanic living in rural areas. The next lowest were Hispanic households in center city areas (NTIA, 1999).

Black and Hispanic households are half as likely to have a computer at home than White non-Hispanic and Asian/Pacific Islander non-Hispanic households. The computer gap between Whites and Blacks has increased from 16.8 percentage points in 1994 to 23.4 in 1998. For Whites and Hispanics, the gap has increased from 14.8 percentage points in 1994 to 21.1 percentage points in 1998 (NTIA, 1999). Thus, it is clear not only that the gap exists, but also that it is increasing.

By Race or Ethnic Group and Income
While race and ethnicity are important determinants of whether or not a household has a computer, income appears to be as significant, if not more so. In 1998, more than three-fourths of the households of all racial and ethnic groups with annual income of $75,000 or more had a computer at home. On the other hand, less than one-fifth of households of all racial/ethnic groups with income of less than $15,000—except Asian-Pacific Islanders non-Hispanic—had a computer (NTIA, 1999).

By Education Level
Whether or not a household has a computer is closely linked with level of education. Almost 70 percent of those with a bachelor's degree or higher had a computer in 1998, whether they lived in rural or urban areas or the center city. Approximately one-third of those with a high school diploma or GED had a computer compared to 15 percent of those who had some high school. Less than one-tenth of the households with only an elementary education had a computer (NTIA, 1999).

Across the country, those with a bachelor's degree or higher are more than eight times as likely to have a computer than those with an elementary school education. In rural areas, the disparity is much larger; those with a bachelor's degree are eleven times more likely to have a computer as those with only an elementary education (NTIA, 1999).

By Household Type
More than 60 percent of all households consisting of married couples with children younger than 18—with the exception of those living in the

center city—had a computer at home. Among households headed by a female with children younger than 18, less than one-third had a computer; a little more than one-fourth of these female-led households living in the center city had a computer (NTIA, 1999).

Nonfamily households were least likely to have a computer; a little over a fourth of these families had a computer, with those living in the rural areas being the least likely to have a computer—only 18.1 percent (NTIA, 1999).

By Age and Region
More than half of all households between the ages of 35 and 55 years of age had a computer, while only one-fourth of those 55 years old or older had one. Approximately one-third of those under 25 years had a computer at home. Almost half of the households in the Western U.S. had a computer, compared to 40 percent of the other three regions (Northeast, Midwest, and South) (NTIA, 1999).

Households Using the Internet

The use of the Internet increased significantly between 1994 and 1998, but the gap between those who have access and those who do not also increased. The factors that influence whether a household has a computer at home also play an important role in access to the Internet (NTIA, 1999).

By Income
Approximately 60 percent of households with income of $75,000 or more used the Internet from home in 1998. Less than 10 percent of households with income of less than $20,000 use the Internet (NTIA, 1999).

By Race or Ethnic Group
A little more than one-tenth of all Hispanic and Black non-Hispanic households used the Internet in 1998, compared to almost 30 percent of White non-Hispanic and 36 percent of Asian/Pacific Islander households (NTIA, 1999).

The gap between White, Black, and Hispanic households increased from 1997 to 1998. In 1997, the gap between White and Black households was 13.5 percentage points; by 1998, the gap had grown to 18.6 percentage points. The gap between White and Hispanic households grew from 12.5 percentage points in 1997 to 17.2 percentage points in 1998 (NTIA, 1999).

By Race or Ethnic Group and Income
Income seems to be a more important factor than race or ethnicity in relation to the use of the Internet. In 1998, almost half of all households with income of $75,000 used the Internet. More than 60 percent of White families used the Internet, while less than ten percent of White, Black and Hispanic households with incomes of less than $15,000 used the Internet in 1998 (NTIA, 1999).

By Education
Almost one-half of all households with an earned bachelor's degree or higher used the Internet in 1998. Approximately 15 percent of households with a high school diploma used the Internet, but only one in six of those with less than a high school diploma did. Those with a bachelor's degree or higher are nearly 16 times as likely to have access to the Internet from home as those with only an elementary education (NTIA, 1999).

By Household Type
Fifteen percent of the households with a female head of household and with children under 18 years of age used the Internet in 1998. Those in the center city used it least—only 13 percent, compared to almost 40 percent of the households of married couples with children younger than 18. And almost one-fifth of male householders with children younger than 18 used the Internet (NTIA, 1999).

By Age and Region
In 1998, more than one-third of the households between the ages of 35 and 54 used the Internet. One-fifth of those younger than 25 and less than 15 percent of those older than 55 years of age used the Internet. About one-fourth of the families in the Northeast, Midwest, and South used the Internet in 1998, while almost one-third of the households used the Internet in the West (NTIA, 1999).

Community College Students: A Profile

American community colleges have been described as the Ellis Island to higher education because of their open door admissions policy, easy geographic access, and affordable tuition. By 1998, the 1,132 U.S. community colleges enrolled 5.4 million students in credit courses. In addition, it is estimated that an equal number take noncredit classes. Approximately 46 percent of all first-time college freshmen enroll in community colleges. Forty-nine percent of all undergraduates who are members of minority groups are enrolled in community colleges, while minority students represent about 30 percent of all community college students. Furthermore, over half—55 percent—of all American Indians and Hispanics enrolled in higher education attend community colleges. About 45 percent of all African American undergraduates are enrolled in community colleges. By 1997, more Hispanic students than African American students were enrolled in the community colleges: 637,813 Hispanic and 599,586 African Americans (Phillippe, 2000).

In 1997, 46 percent of community college students attended school part time, principally because of work and family responsibilities. Approximately 36 percent of the students work full time. About 60 percent were older than 22 years of age; 15 percent were 40 years old or older. In addition, approximately one-third were between 18 and 22 years old, and only 4 percent were younger than 18 (Phillippe, 2000).

A significant majority of community college students—58 percent of the total in 1997—are female. Of those 40 years old or older, 65 percent were female, and almost 63 percent of the female students were enrolled as part-time students (Phillippe, 2000).

While nearly 90 percent of students who enroll in four-year colleges or universities take either the SAT or the ACT, only about 40 percent of community college students do so. Community college students are more likely to score in the lowest quartile—43 percent—and only 10 percent score in highest quartile (Coley, 2000).

Community college students are more likely to have one or more of the major factors shown by research to put degree-seeking students at risk. In 1995-96, almost one-half of the community college students delayed their entry to college, compared to less than one-fifth of those who attended either private or public four-year institutions (Coley, 2000).

Financial concerns are important to community college students, many of whom come from the lower socioeconomic classes. Findings from a recent survey indicate that more than 60 percent of the community college students polled identified personal financial problems and the cost of books and materials as problems associated with taking college classes. One-half of the community college students surveyed listed the cost of childcare and the cost of a computer as important barriers (Phillippe & Valiga, 2000).

When comparing the have-nots in the Digital Divide with the description of community college students, the overlap is clear. Indeed, the demographic and social profile of those most negatively impacted by the Digital Divide is almost identical to common cohorts of community college students—minority, rural, low income, and the academically underprepared. Clearly, the community colleges are, in fact, enrolling many of the students who have the least access to the information and communication technologies that are driving the new global economy.

Knocking at the Open Door: More Students, More Diversity

Recent reports on projections of high school graduation and college enrollment indicate two major trends: more students will be knocking at the open door of the community colleges, and they will be more diverse than ever.

High School Graduate Projections

In 1998, the Western Interstate Commission for Higher Education (WICHE) and The College Board published a projection report of high school graduates by state and race or ethnicity to 2012. Using 1995-96 as the base year, they projected that the total number of high school graduates in the United States will increase from 2,292,031 in 1995-96 to 2,768,828 in 2012, representing a 12.1 percent increase.

The number of African-American public high school graduates is projected to increase by 23.9 percent from 298,957 in 1995-96 to 370,393 in 2012. African Americans represented 13 percent of the public high school graduates in 1995-96, and they are projected to represent 13.6 percent in 2012 (WICHE & The College Board, 1998).

Native American public high school graduates are projected to increase from 20,673 in 1995-96, when they represented .09 percent of the graduates, to 36,214 in 2012, when they will make up 1.31 percent of the total graduates—or an increase of 75.2 percent (WICHE & The College Board, 1998).

Asian/Pacific Islander public high school graduates will almost double, from 100,921 in 1995-96 to 194,984 in 2012, an increase of 48 percent. By 2012, they will represent 7.04 percent of the total graduates, compared to 4.4 percent in 1995-96 (WICHE & The College Board, 1998).

A dramatic 58 percent increase in Hispanic public high school graduates is projected, from 218,358 in 1995-96 to 517,746 in 2012. In 1995-96, Hispanic graduates made up 9.53 percent of the graduates; by 2012, they will represent 18.7 percent (WICHE & The College Board, 1998).

White non-Hispanic high school graduates will actually decrease, from 1,653,122 in 1995-96 to 1,649,491 in 2012. They will represent less than 60 percent of all the high school graduates in 2012, compared to 72.12 percent in 1995-96 (WICHE & The College Board, 1998). These figures underscore that the number of high school graduates in the U.S. is increasing, yet most of the growth is occurring in minority populations.

College Enrollment Projections

By 2015, college enrollments will increase by 2.6 million. This growth in undergraduate enrollment is driven by a number of factors; the most important of these is children born between 1965 and 1982, who will generate 1.7 million more undergraduate students by 2015 (Carnevale & Fry, 2000).

The return of older students to college, along with increasing immigration, will result in an additional 850,000 students. More than one-half of the increase (53.5 percent) in undergraduates will be concentrated in five states, with California experiencing the largest number: 730,000. The other four states and the number of undergraduates projected are Texas with 310,000, Florida with 190,000, New York with 110,000, and Arizona with 90,000. Of the projected 2.6 million students, 1.43 million will be in these five states (Carnevale & Fry, 2000). By 2015, 14 states will account for three-fourths of the increase in undergraduate enrollment.

Racial and Ethnic Mix: More Diversity
The racial and ethnic mix of the students who will be enrolled in college by 2015 will be very diverse. The majority of the students in three states—Hawaii, California, and New Mexico—and the District of Columbia will be majority-minority, and almost half of the undergraduates in Texas will be minority students.

In fact, African Americans, Hispanic, and Asian/Pacific Islanders will account for 80 percent of the increase in undergraduate enrollment; however, the rate of growth will differ among these groups.

African Americans
African American undergraduate enrollments are projected to increase by 400,000 by 2015, and will represent approximately 13 percent of the total number of undergraduates, a modest increase. The four states with the largest projected increase in African American students are Texas with 50,000; Florida and Georgia with 40,000 each; and Maryland with 30,000 (Carnevale & Fry, 2000).

Asian/Pacific Islanders
The largest percentage increase in undergraduate enrollment in 2015 will come from Asian/Pacific Islanders—86 percent. The number of Asian/Pacific Islanders enrolled in college will increase from 700,000 in 1995 to 1.3 million is 2015, or an increase of 600,000. More than half of these students will be in California (Carnevale & Fry, 2000).

Hispanic Students
The largest absolute increase in college enrollment will come from Hispanic students, whose numbers will grow from 1.4 million undergraduates in 1995 to 2.5 million in 2015. Four states will account

for two thirds of the increase in Hispanic undergraduates. About 36 percent of the increase in Hispanic enrollment in these four states—216,000 students—will occur in California. Texas, Florida, and New York (Carnevale & Fry, 2000).

White Majority
    The increase in White non-Hispanic students will be modest, from 9.5 million in 1995 to 10 million. However, the percentage of White students, in comparison to the total, will decrease, from 70.6 percent in 1995 to 62.8 percent in 2015 (Carnevale & Fry, 2000).

Conclusion

    The Digital Divide, the gap between those who have access to digital communications and information technologies and those who do not have this access, is in some ways a racial ravine. However, factors such as income, age, household type, and geography also play a role in defining the gap between digital haves and have-nots. African-American and Hispanic families are half as likely to have a computer at home as White non-Hispanic and Asian/Pacific Islander families. Approximately one-tenth of African-American and Hispanic families have access to the Internet from home compared to more than 40 percent of White non-Hispanic families, and the gap is increasing.

    The profile of the 5.4 million students served by community colleges is very similar to those families who have less access to computers and the Internet. Projections of high school graduates and college enrollment indicate that both will increase in the next ten to fifteen years and that the students who will enroll in college will be much more diverse than ever before in this country.

    African-American enrollment will show a modest increase while Asian/Pacific Islanders will grow the fastest. However, Hispanics will have the largest increase in terms of absolute numbers; in fact, by 2015 more Hispanics will be enrolled in higher education than African Americans.

    In the pages that follow, good colleagues from community colleges nationally and internationally share their strategies to address these demographic changes and technology imperatives. In the concluding chapter, we take a final look at the role of community colleges and the Digital Divide and suggest further avenues for research, action, and exploration.

REFERENCES

Carnavale, A. P., & Fry, R. A. (2000). *Crossing the Great Divide: Can We Achieve Equity When Generation Y Goes to College?* Princeton, NJ: Educational Testing Service.

Coley, R. J. (2000). *The American Community College Turns 100: A Look at Its Students, Programs, and Perspectives.* Princeton, NJ: Educational Testing Service.

National Telecommunications and Information Administration (NTIA) (1999). *Falling Through the Net: Defining the Digital Divide. A Report on the Telecommunications and Information Technology Gap in America.* Washington, DC: U.S. Department of Commerce.

Phillippe, K. A., & Valiga, M. J. (2000). *Faces of the Future: A Portrait of America's Community College Students.* Washington, DC: American Association of Community Colleges.

Phillippe, K. A. (Ed.). (2000). *National Profile of Community Colleges: Trends and Statistics* (3rd ed.). Washington, DC: American Association of Community Colleges.

Western Interstate Commission for Higher Education & The College Board. (1998). *Knocking at the College Door.* Boulder, CO: WICHE Publications.

CHAPTER 3

TECHNOLOGY-BASED
OCCUPATIONAL EDUCATION PROGRAMS:
SHORT-TERM TRAINING
WITH LASTING ADVANTAGES

Stella Perez

Within the world of physics, there exists a natural law called the Angle of Repose. According to this principle, two lines intersect at a degree of perfect balance such that an object may rest above in a state of equilibrium. This point of equalization is known as the Angle of Repose. Within a social order of human beings, such balances of perfection may seem impossible to achieve, but the understanding of dependence and balance as constructs of social concordance are fundamental beliefs of America's system of public education.

American history reveals Jeffersonian principles of democracy and social well-being as the theoretical underpinnings of public education. In theory, the philosophy of education for all was based on the belief that standardization of language, systemization of literacy, and uniform social behavior would build a strong and coherent foundation of new government. In practice, standardization, homogenization, and assimilation were the primary social tenets of American public education. The same principles that were to move education from aristocracy and meritocracy to democracy tended to offer the privilege of information and knowledge to a broader population base, but all too often the limits of this expansion were drawn along well-established lines defined according to color, ethnicity, and race. Social conventions and economic realities have repeatedly and disproportionately enabled White males, from the end of the American Revolutionary war through the Morrill Land Grant era to the passage of the GI Bill to benefit from higher educational advancement and technical training achievement.

Progress has been made through policy and legislation to offset our history's prevailing consequences of preference and unequal opportunity.

Within the past three decades, minority groups have made significant gains in educational status and career advancement. In spite of these gains, today's culmination of demographic shifts, global economics, and technological transformation prompt new questions, new issues, and new ideas in the face of old social barricades. In particular, these forces are converging to reopen the gap—to upset the balance in the Angle of Repose—between society's haves and have-nots.

Short-Term Programs for Lifelong Learning

The American Dream has been cast in the light of higher education institutions. The college diploma has prevailed as the calling card of privilege and access to expansive career opportunity. Social status has long been correlated with Carnegie classification, with those attending private tier-one institutions of higher education ranked highest, followed by those credentialed by more accessible, but still well-regarded public institutions. Recently, however, these well-traveled paths to success have been altered drastically by technological innovation, the unbounded global economy, and changing demographics, forces now casting shadows over the bright lights of alma mater and tradition.

Business leaders, global economists, and policy developers recognize access to information, technological proficiency, and transferable knowledge resources as the requisite skills necessary to navigate a technologically-advanced economy. In the most robust economy our country has seen in more than a century, information technology industries are exploding, and these international companies offer prime wages for technical skills. Prevailing ideas and the historical clout of the baccalaureate degree are coming into question as the demands for skilled information technology (IT) professionals gain momentum against more traditional and general education college programs. The currency in this new technological marketplace is skills, not credentials.

American community colleges have a longstanding legacy of bridging higher education resources to culturally diverse populations. As part of their five-pronged mission—academic transfer, occupational education, remedial and compensatory education, community development, and continuing education—American community colleges extend an open door offer to obtain skills, gainful employment, and career advancement to the broadest segment of the population. In effect, community colleges stand as the threshold of opportunity for the most diverse student population, offering the most gainful skills demanded today. Through creative practice and unconventional theory, two progressive community colleges offer new models for training, developing, and preparing a range of students for success in today's information-based society.

Pima Community College

With more than 60,000 students, Pima Community College (PCC) in Tucson, Arizona, is the fourth largest multicampus community college in the nation. Established in 1966, PCC comprises five campuses that offer traditional academic programs, community development services, and concurrent enrollment opportunities for the local high schools. Its sixth campus, Community Campus, is focused on alternative methods for delivering educational services, including distance learning courses, business and professional training, and short-term technical certification programs.

As with most community colleges, the diversity of history, ethnicity, and economic development of PCC's service area are reflected within the college's student population. Tucson is home to one of the oldest and most rooted Native American Tribes. The Yauqui Indians trace their ancestry to the ancient Anasazi band, who are known as some of the first settlers of the Southwest region. Another local cultural stronghold is the tiny, independently incorporated city of South Tucson. Nested within the city limits of Tucson, the city of South Tucson is one of the state's oldest barrios and has a population base that has historically remained more than 90 percent Hispanic.

The diversity of the city also extends to industry. Tucson houses one of the country's largest military bases, Davis Monthan Air Force Base, which has boosted local employment and built the East Valley's service industries for more than thirty years. The local university, The University of Arizona, has strong ties with NASA and is renowned as a leader in optical science and engineering research. These foundations with government, business, and education, coupled with its sunbelt, have made Tucson a prime location for new technology development and computer-based industries.

In response to this great diversity, PCC has recognized numerous opportunities to bridge local workforce demands with an increased supply of knowledgeable, qualified, well-trained professionals from the great ethnic mix of the local population. The chancellor invites all community members to participate in these opportunities by emphasizing that PCC's approach to learning is never one size fits all, but rather one in which students are offered a mix of options and opportunities to learn according to their own needs and interests. These customized service approaches have led PCC Community Campus to partner with a private corporation, the Industry Training Credit Approval Process (ITCAP), as an authorized technical education center to grant college credit for coursework leading to industry/vendor certification. Examples of these certifications include Microsoft Certified Solution Developer (MCSD), Oracle Database Administrator (Oracle DBA), and Certified Lotus Professional (CLP). Through the ITCAP program, PCC students may enroll in these high-demand, short-term training programs, receive college credit, and jump-start their career advantages. The goals of the program include increasing access to technology training and "opening up new possibilities for students and employers," along with academic support services, financial aid options, and degree articulation opportunities.

These short-term programs target first generation college students who must work to offset the costs of their education, working professionals with family responsibilities that tie them to salary and insurance commitments, and workers in need of skill upgrades before they are replaced by technical innovation. Through ITCAP services, anytime-anyplace learning options, and student support services, PCC is able to couple high-quality instruction with practical skill-based training and offer new avenues of access and opportunity to those unable to travel the traditional, lock-step, four-year academic route to higher education.

St. Petersburg Junior College

As the oldest community college in Florida, St. Petersburg Junior College (SPJC) is witnessing the strongest economy and lowest unemployment rate recorded in over 20 years. Within the Tampa Bay region, information technology industries are exploding, and these companies offer prime wages for technical skills. Growth in the high-tech marketplace has outpaced the workforce, leading to competition beyond product development. The acquisition and retention of technical professionals is a growing concern, with a short supply of information technology workers in a high-demand market. These organizations are looking to educational providers—whether public or private—to train and develop more individuals in ever-branching fields of technology, and they are pulling educational and training institutions into this competitive arena.

SPJC has long served the nontraditional college student and has been an avenue to success for returning adult learners, both first generation college enrollees and full-time employees who can invest only part-time resources into their education. Many of these students come from underserved minority populations. Longstanding experience and evidence from the competitive workforce environment confirm the convictions of SPJC college leaders that the traditional degree pathway may not work for students who come to the community college with an urgency to obtain skills and become immediately employable or advance in their existing careers.

SPJC has responded to this skill-hungry marketplace by developing an array of short-term certificate programs that follow an inverted degree design, integrate flexible course scheduling, and offer high-demand technical skills training as a response to the demands of business and industry. The college has worked closely with local workforce development boards and welfare reform advisors and has relied on extensive market analysis to design programs that meet workforce needs and student goals for immediate employment, but also serve as a first step toward an Associate of Science degree.

The new certificate programs are 18- to 24-credit hour programs that couple basic degree requirements with specialty skills oriented to the latest innovations in industry training, with particular attention given to new developments in information technology. Courses are closely calibrated to business and industry standards and are offered during evenings and weekends as well as in other flexible formats. Unlike traditional sequencing, this inverted degree plan allows students first to complete a one-year certificate training sequence and get immediate experience in their field of study before taking general education courses.

Internships and work-related activities serve as an integral part of these certificate programs, and student services are also an important part of the student's educational experience. Financial aid, tuition reimbursement, and career and counseling services are offered as part of a formative development plan for all students. In addition, one-stop opportunities to complete the full enrollment process for certificate programs are offered through campus-based Information Sessions. SPJC Information Sessions were developed as a direct outreach effort to connect with the busy adult learner population that certificate programs serve best. At these sessions, faculty make presentations throughout the evening. At designated booths, students can meet individually with instructors and review prerequisites and course expectations. Campus counselors are on hand to answer questions related to financial aid application, credit reimbursements, and career planning. During the sessions, the registrar's office is open to enroll students on the spot so they can avoid daytime lines. SPJC recognizes the particular demands and opportunities in this new era of work, and sees its certificate programs as beneficial for many constituents who might not otherwise have such access or opportunity.

Conclusion

In this new era of work, if you are not educated and well trained, technology tends to replace you.

—Former Secretary Robert Reich
(January 1998)

There is amplified warning and much postulation regarding computer access, the pace of technological evolution, and new demands for workforce development. All too often, these forecasts and mandates fail to include our society's traditional have-nots or minority populations and the impact of their population growth in the new digitally-driven century. Although most agree that access is the answer to bridging the Digital Divide, few recognize that a complexity of need, opportunity, and balance among access to technology tools extends beyond the availability of resources. This dilemma reaches into fundamental and historical barriers that have separated, tracked, and granted gainful advantage to some groups over others in educational institutions and beyond.

Pima Community College and St. Petersburg Junior College are models of institutions moving past the warnings, postulation, and assumptions toward action. By challenging existing standards and customs, PCC and SPJC have transformed traditional process and practice into opportunities for a greater population of new learners. Access to technology-based programs is only one part of the myriad outreach services and options available through their initiatives. The programs highlighted here are not stand-alone programs buried within college catalogs. Instead, the leaders of these institutions promote and support multiple efforts to offer short-term occupational education opportunities through flexible service-based programs to a greater spectrum of students. This commitment paves the way for many community members who were once excluded to travel the lucrative path of technology promise and productively engage in the next generation of work. It is this dedication to the ideals of democratic education in progressive community colleges that offers hope for moving the sides of today's Digital Divide into an Angle of Repose—and for making the American Dream available to all members of society in the Digital Age.

CHAPTER 4

BRIDGING THE DIGITAL DIVIDE: SUPPORTING THE LEARNING JOURNEY OF COLLEGE FACULTY AND STAFF

Ruth Mclean

The Information Age is affecting colleges in dramatic ways. Students arrive with a wide range of computer skills and knowledge, staff are required to use software to perform job tasks and to communicate with others, and faculty are required to know software or hardware as a subject of instruction and as a tool to deliver instruction and support student learning. In addition, research and communication, major functions in an academic institution, are conducted electronically.

Many of the same transformational changes of the Information Age that are dramatically changing community college instruction have also resulted in a Digital Divide between those with access to information technology (IT) and the tools required for computer and Internet literacy, and those without IT access and tools. These continual changes with and to technology require that all members of the college community be continual learners. Humber College of Applied Arts and Technology in Toronto, Ontario, has created a professional development facility that supports the learning journey of faculty and staff as they bridge the Digital Divide.

Humber College includes "enabled employees" as a value statement within the college mission statement. Today, an enabled employee is one who possesses the ability to use computers, computer peripherals, the Internet, and other emerging technologies on the job. Several years ago, three strategic decisions were made at Humber to actualize this concept of enabled employees:

1. All professional development programs and activities would be aligned with the goals, directions, and plans of the college.

2. The professional development department would retain the lead in technology training.
3. Computer training would be integrated into the professional development program.

As a result of these strategies, Humber's professional development department began providing teaching, learning, and curriculum consulting services and workshops with a specific focus on addressing new educational trends. New technologies became part of the program when the first microcomputers, PETS, were introduced. Faculty pioneers experimented with these PETS, but we were not able to meet the needs and interests of a majority of staff until Windows-capable computers became widely available. Because the technology training remains in the professional development department, teaching faculty are responsible for developing and presenting workshops. This factor has improved the credibility of the training since teaching strategies and classroom anecdotes are included in the discussions.

These strategic decisions also led to a new philosophy and approach to professional development that was fostered to help prepare and support technology-enabled employees at Humber. As digital training became a critical professional development activity, the decision was made to present technology as just another teaching tool rather than a special item. The focus—strongly supported by faculty—was not on technology, but on the application of software to the learning or business process.

We envisioned an outcome in which all faculty would have a full range of teaching and information technology skills from which to select instructional strategies to support student learning. Furthermore, we envisioned all employees with a full set of current information technology skills and resources from which to choose to undertake tasks and to communicate with students and with each other.

The Studio: A One-Stop Resource for Instructional Technology Support

As interest in learning and using new technologies grew, we realized that Humber had several distinct but related physical centres (computer training, graphics, consulting services) providing instructional support to faculty. Faculty were required to visit several wings and floors of the college for help, often losing momentum and enthusiasm. The staff of the centres had the same problem. We envisioned a central location for all faculty and staff to access all the programs and services we offered; such a centre would increase our effectiveness and efficiency. With the development of the Instructional Support Studio, the one-stop resource centre became a reality. The Studio, as it became known, brings together staff and equipment involved in a range of professional development, staff computer training, graphic and audio/visual production, online learning, and multimedia development activities.

Purpose

With the focus on learning, the Studio supports the work of any staff member by providing a range of learning activities as well as a place to expand one's network, meet with others, acquire resources, and use high-end equipment. Every effort is made to support faculty in the creation of learning materials or the exploration of new instructional strategies. The Studio is a designed to enable faculty and staff to improve their technology skills and their understanding of instructional technology.

Physical Facilities

The Studio occupies three interconnected rooms: a computer training lab with eight networked computers and projection unit; a large, open area with five high-end computers including peripherals such as scanners, CD burners, digital tablets, and zip drives; and the work room of the college graphics department. Staff offices line the large, open area so users have easy access to assistance. No one in the college is required to come to the Studio, so we strive for friendly, learning-focused service in an atmosphere that encourages faculty to learn, work, and experiment on a drop-in, just-in-time, or scheduled basis.

Philosophy

Learning is central to everyone and everything in the Studio. To encourage staff learning, we developed a multifaceted program with multiple activities and methodologies. We know that staff have different learning styles, needs, and schedules; therefore, we strive to be available when staff members have the need for just-in-time learning. We know that not all staff will relate equally with all Studio staff, so we have a range of people, knowledge, skills, and personalities available.

Staffing
The three or four official faculty consultants in the Studio serve part time on release from their departments. Each consultant has a teaching responsibility and a distinct set of skills and knowledge. The consultants offer workshops, provide consulting skills, and act as coaches and mentors to those interested in learning. We also have a range of unofficial consultants—staff and faculty who have special skills they want to share. One technician assists staff with the high-end equipment, administers the online courses, and works with the technology pioneers, often developing innovative solutions to technical challenges when instructional material is being developed.

In addition, a co-op student from a local university acts as a lab assistant who is available when the lab is open. The lab assistant conducts workshops, is available for individual appointments or general assistance, and revises or writes workshop handouts. When needed, Humber students are hired to assist faculty on special Studio projects.

Activities
All Studio activities are developed and evaluated by referring to the mission and plans of the college and college departments; Studio activities must visibly support these directions. Some reference to or use of technology is integrated in the traditional professional development programs for new or part-time faculty, as well as in curriculum, evaluation, learning strategies, and customized workshops. A variety of Studio activities are targeted specifically for information technology:

Studio Workshops cover a range of topics, including such offerings as word processing, Web searching, Web page or website development, and online teaching. Application of the software or product to learning or classroom activities is woven into the workshops, and formal and informal needs assessments help identify future workshop topics. In 1999, the Studio served over 1,042 registrants in the 237 workshops offered.

Customized Workshops are designed for specific groups of staff on request. A department may have new equipment, upgraded software, new staff, or a technology-driven learning need. The Studio meets that need through specially focused training in these customized workshops.

Individual Coaching is provided by the lab assistant or faculty consultants and is available by appointment. This coaching is particularly helpful to faculty whose schedules and learning needs do not coincide with scheduled Studio activities. It also provides additional assistance to staff who find the workshops do not meet their particular needs. With over 500 individual appointments a year, the lab assistant often develops support relationships with staff members that lead to ongoing appointments and learning.

Studio Projects are partnerships developed among faculty, the Studio, the faculty members' department, and students. In a project, defined as the development or revision of teaching or curriculum material to digital format, much time is spent in the conversion—inputting text, scanning graphics, or learning software. Faculty time, however, is often more valuably spent designing the curriculum and learning activities. With support from partners in a Studio project, a faculty member can concentrate on pedagogy while other members of the team focus on the technical details.

The faculty member meets with a Studio consultant to articulate the project; they agree on the components, discuss the details, and determine the feasibility of the project. The faculty member completes a brief project proposal form, and, to ensure that the project is aligned with department goals and objectives, the faculty member's academic administrator is asked to approve the project. Ownership of the material is discussed at this time.

In a project coordinated by a Studio consultant, the Studio provides up to 20 hours of student assistance to the faculty member. If the project requires more than 20 hours of student time, the department head may agree to complete the project out of the department's budget. Fortunately, projects have never been turned down because of extended completion projections. Throughout the project, Studio consultants coordinate and monitor the effort by locating resources, providing student assistance, supplying assistance with curriculum or learning design, and scheduling meetings with the student and faculty member. Studio projects may involve a number of detailed steps and include activities such as those in the following list:

- Combine and edit two videotapes of the student robotic competition to create a three to four minute clip suitable for uploading to a website.
- Scan slides or pictures for use in faculty presentations to be uploaded to a database or burned onto a CD.
- Add sound to PowerPoint presentations.
- Develop a website for instruction.
- Convert student exercises to Web format and upload to a website.
- Convert a test bank to a format compatible with WebCT.
- Digitize graphic drawings, maps, and diagrams.
- Convert paper and electronic files to Web pages.
- Convert typed manuals to electronic format.

Drop-Ins or Appointments are available in the lab and for the high-end equipment for practice or production. The office staff has developed a number of technical assistance skills and often help faculty get started.

Help Documents distributed to all workshop attendees are also available to those who prefer to learn on their own. Others access the documents from the Studio website, which includes other online references and customized documentation relating to specific software.

Online Help Instructions for using the peripheral equipment are available for independent learning or for use when Studio staff are not available.

Vendor Demonstrations are arranged several times a year and often relate to hardware or software advancements. Demonstrations of learningware and online curriculum are a current focus.

Certification is important for some college staff. Studio staff have developed short evaluative exercises and purchased commercial software for evaluating specific skills. These certificates are used by support and human resources staff to identify specific skills.

Sponsoring Registration for online conferences is extremely useful for faculty and staff, especially regarding the annual Community College Teaching Online Conference. Before and after the conference, the Studio arranges for participants to form a support network and identify learning needs. These conferences also give Studio staff an opportunity to identify issues, new trends, faculty needs, and various reactions to online learning.

Sponsorship to Conferences is an important professional development opportunity for faculty, staff, and administration. In conjunction with the president or academic vice president, the professional development department administers the college budget for technology conferences. After criteria are developed for those who wish to present or participate, Studio staff assist with the development of the written proposals and manage the logistics for submission and attendance. Attendees meet both before and after conferences to share goals and experiences.

Hot Bytes is the Studio newsletter and is published three or four times a year. Using a concise form the staff calls bytes, the Studio provides condensed information on new activities, programs, and equipment to a college staff that is often too busy to read long, detailed articles. Contact information is provided for readers who want to learn more, and staff are encouraged to contribute. Along with announcements, interviews, and a technology joke or two, a typical issue *Hot Bytes* might include items on topics such as new software or hardware acquisitions, interesting Internet sites, library or IT department activities, and tips for using technology as a teaching and learning tool.

Resources, including an expanding collection of manuals, books, CDs, and other publications, are available in the Studio or on the website, and a supply of clip art and graphics are accessed regularly.

User Groups and Listservs are frequently developed and receive support as needed. Currently, the most active group is the user group for online instruction.

Studio Access and Use is designed to meet various information technology learning needs and is open to all Humber employees. Part-time faculty use the Studio as a learning and production facility since they often have difficulty accessing equipment in their departments. As they get to know the Studio and its services better, they spread the word in their departments.

The Studio does not place strict limits on technology use, nor do Studio staff monitor use closely. For example, a faculty member may learn how to use the scanning equipment by scanning family vacation photos. Often, within a few weeks the faculty member is back scanning material for instructional use.

The Studio maintains confidentiality, and records are not sent to the departments. Some participants in Studio activities are embarrassed at their level of learning, while others want to surprise their colleagues with their newly acquired skills. In addition, some support staff are reluctant to let their managers know about their new learning, as this may be perceived as preparation for a new job. Except for Human Resource Department workshops that are related to contractual obligations, attendance is kept for the Studio's statistical use only.

Benefits and Impact

With its focus on learning, this multifaceted program has many benefits. By aligning services with the college mission and goals and by working with all employees at various levels of IT skills and development, the Studio is perceived positively by the members of the campus community. It serves as a provider of resources in a nonthreatening environment that addresses problem solving and supports learning. In the Studio, employees find a comfortable learning space in which innovation and experimentation are encouraged and supported.

A steady stream of staff has accessed Studio resources, experienced faculty have become reenergized and renewed, and part-time faculty have found a place where, surrounded by a learning culture, they are able to absorb the values and culture of the college. Studio consultants seize opportunities to interweave instructional or curriculum design principles and strategies into Studio projects and workshops. Mixing types and levels of staff in workshops expands networks and encourages a better appreciation of various roles in the college. By capitalizing on the willingness of staff to share expertise, the Studio develops a cadre of coaches, mentors, and trainers who add their special focus and styles to the network. They provide informal outreach services for the Studio, identify resources for their colleagues, and detect needs the Studio should address.

Humber College is focused on providing learning opportunities that prepare all its students for success in the workplace. To do that, the faculty and staff must be trained in the variety of activities students will be expected to perform when they join the workforce. As an increasing number of faculty are trained to integrate technology into student learning activities, the anticipated effect is being realized: technology use is increasing across the curriculum. Students who come to Humber having had little or no access now have opportunities to develop and use technology skills in multiple environments and with multiple applications at the college.

In a sense, the Studio's technology training component has helped bridge another kind of Digital Divide—one that exists among faculty with a range of technology training and experience that spans from thorough to none. Designed to meet the diverse instructional technology needs of Humber educators, the Studio has implemented a successful strategy for bridging this faculty divide. If Humber and other community colleges continuously strive to provide opportunities for all faculty and staff to use computers, the Internet, and other emerging technologies, we will be better positioned to meet and exceed the needs of our diverse students, many of whom are trying to reach academic and professional success by crossing the bridge over the Digital Divide.

CHAPTER 5

MARICOPA'S OCTILLO: CONNECTIVITY FOR CURRICULUM, TECHNOLOGY, AND PEDAGOGY

Alfredo G. de los Santos Jr. and Naomi O. Story

Today, the technology revolution is dramatically changing the way we learn and work. With the exponential changes in technology, demands on community colleges in meeting multifaceted needs and requirements for our diverse communities continue to grow and to challenge us in many ways. The knowledge, skills, and values we need to teach change rapidly as students come to us as increasingly sophisticated users of technology and as many faculty members add technology to their pedagogical palettes. In addition, many of our traditional methods for shaping and processing curricula and programs have become archaic and stifling.

As community colleges become the point of entry into higher education for more students with distinctive and differing educational goals, the organization and processes we have put in place often impede changes in curriculum development or lead to barriers that frustrate students and faculty. For example, limited English proficiency community college students may want to acquire computer literacy skills, but they may not have the prerequisite English skills or the time to take a traditional classroom-based course in computer literacy. Another example is the highly computer literate student who enters our system and is expected to take a technology literacy course to fulfill degree requirements. This student has much more knowledge and skill in technology use than some of our faculty have. Frustration also exists among faculty who cannot change the quickly outdated curriculum because it takes so long to process dynamic and relevant technology competencies. Both faculty and students realize that it is difficult for graduates to be competitive and viable in the workforce without completion of meaningful curricula, and that technology is increasingly essential to teaching and learning.

At the Maricopa County Community College District, an initiative know as Ocotillo has been a catalyst for instructional and technological advancement within a large, multicollege system by serving as a responsive and effective organizational change structure for more that 12 years. Ocotillo is a systemic collaboration of faculty, administrators, and staff who are committed to promoting the effective use of instructional technology. Maricopa's Ocotillo initiative draws its name from a Sonoran desert plant that grows multiple long, sweeping branches from a compact base. Several times a year, usually following a rain storm, an ocotillo plant will burst with green leaves and bright red flowers. Broken branches that fall to the ground will often root and sprout into new plants. The long, arching branches of this plant with their self-renewing qualities represent the organic, grassroots approach to addressing Maricopa's issues of how best to use technology for teaching and learning.

Ocotillo reflects an organizational design that involves inclusion, collaboration, shared leadership, timely and relevant planning, and decision making. The Ocotillo model establishes discourse on the curricular and pedagogical relevance of information technologies that is truly focused on learning for the diverse populations Maricopa serves.

As one of the largest community college systems in the country, Maricopa has had the challenge of developing planning systems that allow for differences in awareness, readiness, and acceptance of technology-based pedagogies and curricula among its ten colleges and their numerous constituencies. The effort to encourage all facets of the system's community to be involved, connected, dynamic, collaborative, and nimble has rarely been easy.

Despite the challenge, Ocotillo has evolved over the years into an organizational structure that truly embodies collaborative decision making and shared responsibility among faculty, administration, and staff to solve multilayered issues and challenges that affect learning with and about technology throughout the district. Maricopans have chosen to be involved in creating solutions that are focused, meaningful, and worthwhile to all students at all times for all educational needs.

Ocotillo: Its History and Evolution

Beginning in 1983, Maricopa leadership made a bold commitment to move to a microcomputer-based teaching and learning environment across its colleges. Chancellor Paul A. Elsner and Vice Chancellors Alfredo G. de los Santos Jr. and Ron Bleed led the charge to provide faculty across disciplines with access to the microcomputer revolution. The goal was to transform our culture so that technology would be part of daily life—second nature to everything done at Maricopa to support the educational process.

Extensive resources and support were provided, including comprehensive faculty computer literacy training. Faculty were encouraged and supported to prepare new curricula and to embrace the use and application of new technologies as part of their pedagogy. Centers to foster faculty development and instructional innovation were created at several colleges. Courses and programs were reformed and restructured to take advantage of technology applications to support learning across academic and occupational fields. The hiring process for new faculty included technology-related interview questions and called for examples of technology applications in teaching and learning.

Course management systems for record keeping, classroom management, assessment, and tracking were developed with the microcomputer as the access venue. Electronic communication became our preferred mode of information dissemination and sharing. Technology infrastructures were upgraded at all ten colleges as part of major capital development efforts. Voters supported one of the largest bond elections to ensure technologically based facilities, classrooms, and learning environments. Long before the information superhighway brought technology and learning together in headline news, we integrated bricks and clicks as part of our capital development initiatives.

In 1986, after observing the spread of data network ports across the district, Vice Chancellor for Student and Educational Development de los Santos began to ask questions among instructional leaders. Some of these questions were particularly challenging to faculty and administrators:

• What is the instructional agenda for technology?
• Who is in charge of that agenda? Who should be? The faculty or the technology staff?
• What happened as a result of money spent on instructional technology?

- What are the benefits for the students? The faculty? The institution?
- Are we in control of the teaching and learning process, or are we driven or limited by the technology that is available?
- Assuming that major changes will occur in technology that is available to instruction, what do we do now to prepare and make better use of that technology to enhance the process of teaching and learning?

The attempts to respond to these questions led to the creation of Ocotillo, which began in 1987 as a faculty-driven think tank to explore issues related to instructional technology. At that time, Ocotillo involved committees, events, activities, information sharing, and product development to support technological innovation and application across the district.

Each committee was chaired by one to three faculty members and supported by one or two administrative staff members who provided logistical, technical, secretarial, and other support to the faculty. Regular meetings were held to address the questions asked by de los Santos and others that emerged from the discussions. Faculty-led committees also established new curricular structures such as open entry-open exit courses so students could complete technology literacy, software application, and other courses at their own pace.

Standards for technology infrastructure were developed for district facilities and became a national model for technology planning and building specifications. Designs for classrooms of the future and high-tech centers and labs were the result of an Ocotillo committee. The districtwide library automation system was an Ocotillo product and new concepts and ideas emerged that changed forever the role, function, and design of traditional libraries.

Through the decade of the 1990s, Ocotillo helped Maricopa infuse information technologies, instructional innovations, and new pedagogies such as service learning, distance learning, and video conferencing into teaching and learning activities across the district. In addition, Ocotillo had a significant impact on the curriculum.

Curriculum and Technology: Process and Results

The process for curriculum development and modification at the Maricopa Community Colleges through the 1980s can be described as bureaucratic, paper based, time consuming, sequential, and multilayered. A faculty member who wanted to propose a new course, for example, would have to complete a set of forms and attach a document that included the goals of the course and Maricopa's eight common course elements: prefix, number, title, description, prerequisites, credits, student objectives, and brief course outline.

The proposed course would have to be reviewed and approved by the college department, the college curriculum committee, the discipline instructional council made up of the department chairs across the ten colleges, the district curriculum committee, and the governing board, usually in that order. Multiple copies of the proposal had to be made and shared with as many as 75 individuals. The quickest way to distribute the proposal was through the traditional intercollege mail system rather than by e-mail. Approval of such a proposal could take at least six months, and proposals for occupational programs, which require approval at the state level, could take even longer. It was not uncommon for the proposed course data to be entered into databases on four separate occasions, each using a different format.

In the mid-1990s, the curriculum development process was completely re-engineered to reduce the time and effort required. Using Maricopa's technology infrastructure, the process was made digital and server based. Proposed curriculum data are entered only once, the review and approval process is simultaneous, and little if any paper is used. All interested parties have ready access to the information, and any issues are resolved electronically via e-mail. With this new system, the district curriculum committee and the governing board normally approve a curriculum proposal within a month after it leaves the college from which it originated.

Beyond streamlining the process, the impact on the curriculum and course offerings has been very significant. The first effect has been in modularizing the courses, thus making them more responsive to student needs. As of June 2000, Maricopa had 7,968 courses in its course bank, almost doubling from 4,000 courses in 1990. The initiative to break courses into modules has taken two basic forms: assigning a suffix to a module of a parent course or creating new courses from a parent course. For example, a four-credit course in the humanities, HUM 151, would be broken down into four one-credit modules: HUM 151 AA, HUM 151 BB, and so on. Three one-hour modules, each a new course, would be created from a three-credit course.

In June 2000, the course inventory included 3,691 suffix modules from 884 parent courses and 1,452 separate modules from 349 parent courses. The curriculum at Maricopa includes a total of 5,143 modules that derive from 1,233 parent courses. Of the total 7,968 courses in the course inventory, almost two thirds are modules. Many of these modules require students to use computers, and others are designed to teach students how to operate and use software packages. For example, the Maricopa course bank in June 2000 included 224 business and personal computer courses that ranged from one credit to three credits, each focusing on specific software.

The other significant change in the curriculum at Maricopa is the number of courses that are available on an open entry-open exit (OE/OE) basis; that is, students can enroll at any time during the academic year and exit when they meet the specified competencies for the course. Depending on individual college needs and priorities, the number of OE/OE courses ranges from a few to nearly a hundred different offerings; however, each course at Maricopa has established competencies, so each course can potentially be offered as an OE/OE option.

Finally, the graduation requirements have changed and evolved over time to reflect the needs of the students, the rapid changes in the workplace, and the pedagogies used by the Maricopa faculty. As a result of a review of the general education program, the district curriculum committee changed the requirements for graduation in the fall of 1987 to include a course on computer use. This graduation requirement could be met by a number of courses identified by faculty across the disciplines. The focus was on the student knowing how to use a computer for different purposes.

By the fall 1995 semester, the pedagogies used by the faculty had changed so much that the district curriculum committee deleted the computer use course as a graduation requirement. By that time, the vast majority of the faculty required students to use computers, so it was not necessary to require such a course. No student could earn a degree from one of the Maricopa Community Colleges without being technology literate.

Ocotillo's continued influence in the circle of curricular development is reflected in OE/OE course enrollment patterns, which have declined in the last two years. Colleges have reported that students now want online OE/OE course offerings so they do not need to travel to the college computer labs. As Ocotillo has been actively fostering interest in Internet delivery of courses through tools such as WebCT and Blackboard in the last three to five years, faculty at Maricopa colleges are developing and offering more OE/OE courses via this more convenient electronic venue.

Successful Elements of Ocotillo

Participation in Maricopa's Ocotillo structure has evolved from the original focus of techies and technocrats who centered on single issues related to technology-based applications and solutions to a much more diverse group of faculty, administrators, and staff who are interested in broad-based, meaningful dialogues and decision making on college-based and districtwide responses to teaching and learning issues.

Faculty still drive the focus and agendas for Ocotillo. However, administrators are much more involved in implementing decisions and recommendations because they are now key players. Since the focus is on the diverse learning and curricular needs of individual colleges and the communities they serve, as well as the entire district, participation has increased and commitment has grown.

Ocotillo has allowed connections to occur among those who are actively involved across the district. Because communication is defined as a systemic venue, it appears to be nonlinear and nonhierarchical, but dynamic and iterative information can be shared more rapidly through technology-based systems.

Ocotillo also installed an early warning system. This statewide community college system is designed to share plans for creating new occupational education programs. Through a statewide listserv, chief occupational education and academic officers are alerted when a community college proposes the creation of a new occupational education program. As colleges are better connected, increasingly collaborative, and more communicative, they can make better decisions or take more informed risks in addressing curricular and pedagogical needs.

Conclusion

As MCCD faculty and staff have become more sophisticated users of technology, the system and its colleges have become better able to address the needs and demands for a new society. Ocotillo is a proven model that is faculty led and administratively supported. It has evolved and improved continuously so that the organization is not an imposing barrier that impedes changes in response to the requirements of a rapidly changing global economy and local community. Decisions about technology-based curricula and pedagogies that help to narrow the Digital Divide are collaboratively made so that the colleges can focus on significant learning for all students at all socioeconomic levels at all times.

CHAPTER 6

DEVELOPING A TECHNOLOGY PLAN TO
CONTINUOUSLY SUPPORT AND ENHANCE
EFFECTIVENESS IN TEACHING AND LEARNING

Leonardo de la Garza

The Digital Divide is a complex and controversial issue that directly influences the manner in which community college educators serve students. A critical aspect of the Digital Divide complexity involves the challenge of keeping up with rapidly changing technology on community college campuses. If community colleges hope to keep up with technological change and enhance and continuously improve the use of technology in learning and teaching processes, then careful and strategic technology planning is imperative.

Faculty and staff at the Tarrant County College District have made efforts to develop a technology plan that places the continual improvement of technology use in teaching and learning at its core. The institution has embarked on a journey toward laying a strong, strategic foundation to address the technology needs of staff and students and, ultimately, to extend the opportunities of the Digital Age to all members of the community. This community includes four campuses serving over 70,000 unduplicated credit and noncredit students each year. The college district, headquartered in Fort Worth, Texas, has been marked by an exceptional legacy of service and excellence.

Defining, Verifying, and Articulating a Perceived Need for Improving the District's Computing and Information Systems

When in 1997 the governing board hired the third chancellor in the district's 32-year history, the new chancellor immediately noted that the district was in the midst of a financial crisis—due primarily to declining enrollments—which for several years had impeded the ability of the college to adequately support or enhance teaching and learning services. Since the district was using its reserves to fund the annual operating budget, resources were not available for investment in technology and equipment.

As a result of his ongoing environmental scanning and assessment of college operations in 1997 that clarified the financial problems, the chancellor realized the inadequacy of the district's technology support system. An external consultant confirmed and detailed an outdated and inefficient technology infrastructure in dire need of attention. For example, hardware was late 1980s vintage, software was mostly developed in-house, and less than a fourth of the faculty had access to the Internet. Computing support systems and electronic communication across the district were bifurcated along academic and administrative support lines. The two computing support units worked independently of each other, leading to confusion and frustration—especially by the users. With the facts in hand and the challenges made clear, it was time to begin articulating the need for improving the college district's computing and information services system. First, though, the district needed a simple, straightforward conceptual framework that could articulate how a technology plan could be built. Importantly, we affirmed that the strategy needed to rely on the strength and viability that comes from wide participation and inclusion. The primary target groups to be informed and included were the college community of users—faculty, staff, and students—and the governing board. The solution had to have the input of the users and, ultimately, the board would need to participate in outlining funding strategies.

The conceptual framework consisted primarily of three rubrics, each representing one of the three principal areas of service in a community college: teaching and learning, student services, and administrative support. Each rubric included a comprehensive list of pertinent activities and functions. A representative group of users, predominantly faculty, were invited to participate in a meeting to review the conceptual framework and suggest additional activities and functions under each of the three areas of service. Additionally, they were asked to indicate their preference, should they be inclined to volunteer to help build the technology plan, for the service area or areas of the plan on which they wanted to work.

At the initial meeting attended by the chancellor's cabinet, the consultant, and 56 employees, the group reviewed the consultant's and chancellor's reports of findings and discussed the conceptual framework for developing a technology plan. The reports confirmed what most strongly suspected; accordingly, the response was one of polite acknowledgement. The response to the proposed conceptual framework, however, was lively and synergetic. New functions and activities were added to each of the three service areas as participants actively engaged with one another to extend the lists.

When each person indicated an area of preference for working on the plan, few participants chose only one area. Although enthusiasm was obvious and commitment to developing a strong technology plan was implied, the multimillion dollar project would require a substantial revenue stream. Because funding approval for this plan had to come from the governing board, engaging that body in the process was extremely important. While the chancellor and the governing board initiated efforts to develop a funding strategy, the technology planning group proceeded with its work by actively engaging the faculty and staff without making a financial commitment on behalf of the board.

As promised at the initial meeting, a second meeting was convened at the Northeast Campus. Ninety faculty and staff members were invited and, when the final count was taken, 101 had participated. By this time, the conceptual framework was more fully developed and was presented to the group. In addition to the initial three areas of service, the team proposed and explained the creation of organizational groupings and a technology committee. Between June and November 1998, with much visioning, synthesizing, organizing, and conceptualizing, the elements and complementary parts of the technology plan were put in place.

Technology Committee Structure and Responsibilities

As the technology plan began to take form, its central organizing body became the technology committee. At the close of the Northeast Campus planning meeting, the chancellor issued the committee its charge:

The Technology Committee's goal is to develop a districtwide information and computing systems strategic plan that will allow for the acquisition and maintenance of a totally integrated state-of-the-art system that serves the needs of students, faculty, and staff by expanding communication capabilities, enhancing teaching and learning opportunities, and facilitating the use of data to obtain information and foster knowledge.

The committee included six co-chairs, two for each of the three service areas. They were responsible for ensuring that communication was maintained throughout the process. In addition, they were to help provide the final draft of the technology plan. They began the process by reviewing several technology plans from other institutions and discussing the issues with colleagues within and beyond the district. This review phase allowed them to develop a strong insight into the planning process.

To ensure extensive participation, eleven representative cluster groups were established within the three major areas of service. Each group was responsible for examining the functions within their specific cluster. In addition, a process was established that allowed the groups to compile a list of technology-related outcomes, including recommendations for realizing and implementing various options, timetables, and methods of evaluation. Another key element to the overall structure was the use of internal technical consultants assigned to work with the cluster groups. These individuals—most of whom had positions with oversight responsibility for key technical support areas—were responsible for providing assistance. They worked with other assigned consultants and across functional areas.

The committee established a timeline for task completion and held regular meetings. Many cluster groups met weekly, with the co-chairs making regular reports to the committee as a whole. After extensive planning, review, and evaluation, the committee co-chairs submitted the first draft of the technology plan to the chancellor on April 12, 1999.

Implementing the Technology Plan

The administrative team immediately identified critical areas essential for the establishment and implementation of a workable process and agreed on four key tenets to guide their part of the plan. First, they agreed that all basic hardware and software would be standardized. Second, they approved the purchase of a new administrative software package. Third, they made a commitment to provide training for staff and faculty. Fourth, they agreed to enhance and improve the existing computing support system. With these key elements in place, a districtwide inventory of all computer-related equipment was conducted. This inventory provided user information, location and description of equipment, and allowed for the identification of areas with and without proper wiring and connectivity. A project manager was assigned to oversee the computer delivery and installation process. In addition, a committee consisting of representatives from key functional departments, including information systems, academic computing, and physical plant and inventory assisted the project manager in the periodic review of issues and challenges as the project continued to evolve and grow. Then, a four-phase computer equipment delivery and installation process was established which focused on coordination and communication among the major departments involved in the implementation process. To maintain equity, this four-phase process was based on two core elements: (1) the computer's processor (i.e., the type of computer) and (2) connectivity status.

The information compiled from the inventory process was used to place all employees into one of four phases. Each phase was based primarily on the computer's capability or processor type. Individuals without computers were given first priority, and replacement of existing units was dependent upon the computer and its capacity. Any exceptions to this process required review and, if applicable, approval by the chancellor. In addition, a training and installation schedule was developed with the stipulation that faculty and staff had to complete training before receiving a computer.

From the outset, the principal reason for improving the district's technology and computing capacity was to better serve students, so the process for installing computers in laboratories and classrooms followed a different format. Each campus president obtained campus consensus on the priority listing for installations within their campus laboratory and classroom environments, with the only limitation being that proper wiring and network connectivity be in place. Approximately 70 percent of the district's computer installations have occurred in student areas.

Fiscal Resources

Regardless of the focus of an institutional technology plan or the process used to develop it, without financial resources, even the best technology plan cannot be realized. Significant investments need to be made, both initially and on a continuing basis.

In 1998, the Tarrant County College District board of trustees unanimously approved a plan to double the maintenance and operation tax levy. This action generates approximately $40 million per year for implementing the technology plan and providing resources for other institutional needs. For the last two years, the college has invested approximately $10 million to implement the technology plan developed by the faculty and staff. This investment allows the district to add new hardware and software, to upgrade the technology, and to replace obsolete technology.

Conclusion

The complexities and challenges associated with the Digital Divide are far reaching, and they strongly influence critical community college functions and processes, particularly those involving teaching and learning. By developing and implementing a strategic technology plan to enhance and continuously improve the use of technology in teaching and learning processes, the district is taking steps to help bridge the Digital Divide, and the Tarrant County College District technology plan has served the college well. Its development and implementation have been a catalyst for uniting the college family in addressing and meeting information systems and computing services needs, as well as the financial needs of the college. At the same time, in response to the decline in student enrollments, a student recruitment, advisement, and retention plan, developed over the past two years by over 100 faculty and staff, has resulted in steady increases in student enrollments.

Seeking solutions to the challenges inherent in the Digital Divide—technology access and training—the Tarrant County College District used inclusive strategies to solicit input from multiple perspectives and to help ensure viability and support for the technology plan. The final product was backed not only by college employees, but also by the governing board and the community who provide funding. It perhaps is axiomatic that the extent to which we, as community college educators, appreciate that the successful implementation of an innovation such as a technology plan for enhancing teaching and learning is a function of the difficulty of the challenge. The tougher the challenge, the sweeter the sense of accomplishing our purpose. Equally, if not more gratifying, is the opportunity to work with and be challenged by creative, caring, and selfless individuals—the faculty and staff of the college—whose efforts to build and implement the district's technology plan have helped diminish the Digital Divide for our students.

Note: Readers seeking more detail are encouraged to access the comprehensive 147-page technology plan of the college district, which may be found at the Tarrant County College District website, www.tccd.net.

CHAPTER 7

AN URBAN TWO-YEAR CAMPUS
STRIVES TO NARROW THE DIGITAL DIVIDE
THROUGH ACCESS AND PARTNERSHIPS

Alex B. Johnson, Patricia Mintz, Paul Abiola, Erika Bell

In October 1999, several government agencies, including the President's Information Technology Advisory Council, sponsored a conference entitled Resolving the Digital Divide: Information, Access, and Opportunity. The conference highlighted findings from the Falling Through the Net investigations conducted initially in 1995 by the National Telecommunications and Information Administration (NTIA). The latest study, completed in 1999, found that although 26.2 percent of United States households now have Internet access, growing disparities exist between income and education levels, racial and ethnic groups, and location, both urban and rural. Based on these findings, the conference participants were asked to develop community-based solutions to the Digital Divide involving cooperative efforts of government, industry, and community (Le Blanc, 1999).

In these cooperative arrangements, community colleges located in urban neighborhoods become powerful allies with various organizations to narrow the Digital Divide. The involvement of two-year colleges is critical because they have high enrollments of minority students, who are often "digitally disenfranchised" from the rapid advancement in information technology in all aspects of American society (de los Santos Jr. & de los Santos, 2000).

Community college involvement is also critical for the development of the nation's inner-city neighborhoods. Perhaps more damaging than the scarcity of computers in the home, these urban communities often lack the financial and technical resources to support technology availability in traditional educational settings like schools and libraries. This lack of access to up-to-date computers leaves residents isolated from the quality of jobs, educational opportunities, and technological tools they need to be able to contribute to the overall society (Benton Foundation, 1998).

Greater Cleveland, Ohio, is not immune to this condition. According to a recent report from the Center for Regional Economic Issues at Case Western Reserve University, at a time when emerging high-tech industries drive the economy, Cleveland is at a troubling disadvantage because of its mediocre educational standing and urban poverty.

Cuyahoga Community College (CCC) is committed to technology access to enable residents of Greater Cleveland to acquire the technical skills needed for success in their educational and professional pursuits. At its three campuses, through its distance learning facilities and with a range of workforce and economic development programs, CCC serves more than 55,000 credit and noncredit students.

Cuyahoga Community College's Metropolitan Campus

Access to technology to facilitate learning is especially important for students at CCC's Metropolitan Campus. The most diverse among the three CCC campuses, it is located near downtown Cleveland and serves 6,000 credit students reflecting the ethnic and racial makeup of the community. Almost 60 percent of the students are African American, Hispanic, Asian American, or from an international background. The Metropolitan Campus offers an array of educational programs including health careers technology, information/computer technology, and engineering technology. Preparing individuals in these important areas is critical to the economic well being of the community, region, and state, and to the expansion of technology literacy in inner city Cleveland (Thomas, 2000). To accomplish these aims, several initiatives have been launched on the Metropolitan Campus and in the community, including a variety of Technology Learning Centers, resource centers, laboratories, and projects to promote technology use among our constituents.

Campus-Based Access: Technology Learning Centers

To consolidate academic computing resources in state-of-the-art facilities, CCC is constructing Technology Learning Centers (TLC) on each of its three campuses. The TLC's contain instructional laboratories, distance learning classrooms, large open-access areas, and instructional technology development rooms for faculty and staff.

The TLC on the Metropolitan Campus is a 40,000 square foot facility opened in January 1999. Although the college operates many dedicated laboratories in areas such as engineering and computer studies, the TLC is the hub for technology applications to teaching and learning. Most of the 300 full- or part-time faculty use the TLC classrooms and laboratories or obtain assistance from TLC staff in the development of online and other distance learning courses or in the use of technology to augment teaching. New technical programs that can lead to high-wage careers have emerged as a result of the technology and expertise available in the TLC. The most recent additions are microcomputer repair and maintenance, network administration, and software systems technology.

The TLC staff works with almost every educational unit to devise innovative approaches to academic computing. Among these approaches is the Sony language system to teach foreign languages, but which has been modified to teach English as a Second Language (ESL), also. The use of the Sony System in this manner is important since ESL students are a growing segment on the campus. Because of language barriers or economic circumstances, most of our ESL students do not have ready access to computers in their homes and can be counted among those affected by the Digital Divide.

In addition to students and staff, community groups benefit from TLC services. More than 50 organizations comprising public schools, community agencies, and corporations throughout Cuyahoga County have used the TLC for short-term computer literacy programs. The TLC supports initiatives sponsored solely by CCC or in partnership with other institutions to introduce school children from underrepresented groups to the benefits of technology. One of these programs, the Science, Engineering, Mathematics, and Aerospace Academy (SEMAA), is coordinated by the college's workforce and economic development division and is partially funded by NASA's Glenn Research Center at Lewis Field. SEMAA students meet throughout the year on the Metropolitan Campus to engage in hands-on, inquiry-based experiences that strengthen their technical skills. CCC is leading the replication of SEMAA programs at community colleges in ten urban locations throughout America.

Local residents view the TLC as an important resource for accessing the Internet, using e-mail services, and developing basic technology skills. They benefit from an initiative to make the TLC a free point of access to computers for neighborhoods that surround the Metropolitan Campus. This initiative accounts in part for the 72,095 logons at the TLC between summer 1999 and spring 2000. The number represents 2,675 individuals or students largely from minority backgrounds; more than 80 percent were African American, Hispanic, Asian American, or Native American.

Community-Based Partnerships

CCC participates in a number of community-based partnerships with organizations that understand the important role computers play in preparing individuals for successful lives and careers.

Cedar Estates Resource Center

Although some CCC programs are situated in public schools, one is located in a public housing development adjacent to the campus. The placement of computers in the Cedar Estates Resource Center is an outgrowth of the college's collaboration with the Tenants Association of Cedar Estates on the Healthy Neighborhood Partnership Program. In this program, initiated in 1995, CCC nursing students and faculty conduct screenings of preschool children with the assistance of the dental unit at MetroHealth Hospital and the Cleveland Sight Center. Since fall 1999, the Resource Center has helped more than 150 residents develop computer literacy and Internet skills to locate community services, find training opportunities, and establish e-mail accounts. Metropolitan Campus staff provide technical support and introduce the residents to CCC educational opportunities through the college's Web page.

Superior Community Learning Center

The Superior Community Learning Center, operated by the East Cleveland Public Schools and funded by the U.S. Department of Education, focuses partly on the development of computer literacy skills for parents. In East Cleveland, a city of 34,000 residents, the average family income is $7,800, and 37 percent of the city's youth live below federal poverty standards. Beginning fall 2000, the Superior Community Learning Center is helping 175 East Cleveland elementary school children, with the assistance of their parents, excel in science and mathematics. The Metropolitan Campus staff will assist with this effort by introducing at least 50 of these parents to word processing software, electronic reference materials, CD-ROM capabilities, and Internet resources, particularly websites offering advice on studying at home.

Health Careers Center Computer Laboratory

One of CCC's several school-based computer laboratories is located at the Health Careers Center, the magnet high school for allied health programs in the Cleveland Municipal School District. Established in 1999, this laboratory helps students succeed in high school courses while they are concurrently enrolled in CCC allied health programs, particularly licensed practical nursing. In fall 2000, 60 Health Career Center students enrolled at the Metropolitan Campus. Their tuition and fees were funded through Post-Secondary Enrollment Options (PSEO), a statewide program that allows qualified students to enroll in college courses while attending high school.

High-Tech Academy

The High-Tech Academy is a CCC collaborative with two public school districts, Cleveland and Warrensville Heights, that enroll large minority student populations. Opening in fall 2000, the academy is designed to prepare up to 360 sophomores, juniors, and seniors from eight high schools for careers in various technology fields. The students are selected through a competitive admissions process including a formal application, letters of support from teachers, and an interview involving parents.

In this program, students spend progressively more of the school week at the Eastern or Metropolitan Campuses of CCC. Initially, they take courses that help them adjust to college life, refine their study skills, and prepare to use computers extensively for learning. Students can pursue a variety of technical fields: finance and banking services, engineering technology, information technology, computer studies, and business services. When they qualify through PSEO, students can earn additional college credits that substitute for their high school courses and can be applied toward a two-year degree at CCC or transferred to four-year institutions.

An Individualized Development Plan (IDP) based on assessments is prepared for each student. The IDP prescribes remedies for improving academic skills, which are refined in campus and school-based computer laboratories featuring Academic Systems software in mathematics and English. The IDP also describes the student's choice of a technical field and serves as a record of student achievements. In the 11th and 12th grades, students serve internships in business settings representing their technical fields. During this time, students also participate in leadership, cultural, and volunteer activities that contribute to their personal and social growth.

The Academy involves several prominent corporate and community partners. National City Bank Corporation provides resources to establish the computer laboratories, to provide college scholarships, and to assist with developing in students the competencies needed for success in the business world. The Greater Cleveland Growth Association assists with locating internships, and the North Coast Tech-Prep Consortium helps develop the competency-based curriculum in the technical fields.

Alliance+ Internet in Education
Alliance+ Internet in Education is a program directed almost exclusively at professional development of teachers in the Cleveland and East Cleveland public schools and Cleveland Catholic Diocese schools. It is replicated in Arizona with Maricopa Community College District and in Florida with Miami-Dade Community College District. The Cleveland component, coordinated by the Metropolitan Campus of CCC, has the potential to affect over 2,300 teachers and 100,000 students in this area. To date, the program has trained 744 teachers who impact 26,040 students.

Alliance+ is funded by a five-year grant from the U.S. Department of Education for the purpose of developing the abilities of classroom teachers while creating training and support infrastructures designed to have a lasting, systemic impact. Alliance+ provides support materials in a variety of formats, advocates the train-the-trainer outreach model, offers continuous follow-up support, and requires community college involvement in the development of mentor teachers who, in turn, train teachers in their home schools.

The *Savvy Cyber Teacher*™ courses are central to the program. Developed by the Stevens Institute of Technology, these courses help teachers apply the Internet to teaching. Teachers can earn graduate credit for their participation. Other partners include Polaris Career Center, Bank Street College of Education, and the League for Innovation in the Community College.‡

Conclusions

Most recommendations on closing the Digital Divide stress integration of technology into teaching and learning and providing opportunities for families and individuals to experience technology in their communities. Cuyahoga Community College's Metropolitan Campus is proving that the use by residents of its technology rich facilities, either on campus or in the community, is one way an urban two-year institution can help accomplish this objective. When done in collaboration with other organizations, access to technology assists residents in understanding the wide variety of telecommunications opportunities that can enrich them personally and professionally (Phillippe & Valiga, 2000). This approach also facilitates community building. As more members of urban neighborhoods gain access to computers, technology provides the right tools to bring them together for common goals and purposes that serve their interests (Carvin, 2000).

---

‡ Detailed information on Alliance+ is available at www.k12science.org/alliance and in Chapter 8 of this book.

REFERENCES

Benton Foundation (1998). *Losing Ground Bit by Bit: Low-Income Communities in the Information Age*. Washington, DC: Benton Foundation.

Carvin, A. (2000, January/February). Mind the Gap: The Digital Divide as the Civil Rights Issue of the New Millennium. *Multimedia Schools*. (pp. 56–58).

de los Santos, Jr., A. G., & de los Santos, G. E. (2000, February). Community Colleges Bridging the Digital Divide. *Leadership Abstracts 12*(1).

Le Blanc, J. (1999, November). Resolving the Digital Divide. *The Digital Beat*. [Online Serial], 1(19). Available at www.benton.org/ DigitalBeat/DB.111299.html.

Phillippe, K., & Valiga, M. (2000). Faces of the Future: A Portrait of America's Community College Students. Summary Findings. Washington, DC: American Association of Community Colleges.

Thomas, T. (2000). *Transforming Ohio: Creating a Workforce to Spec. A Community College Perspective on Issues and Priorities*. Columbus, OH: Ohio Association of Community Colleges.

CHAPTER 8

PREPARING K-12 TEACHERS IN THE USE OF TECHNOLOGY:
COMMUNITY COLLEGES ADDRESS THE DIGITAL DIVIDE

Edward J. Leach

Never before has a society-transforming revolution developed at the rate of today's digital economy. The Internet, the global network of computers, is doubling in size every year, while the World Wide Web, the information that sits on top of the Internet, doubles in size every 90 days. The world has reached our desktop computers and this expansion has transformed businesses, initiated policy reform, and redefined global markets.

In spite of the tremendous impact of technology on today's society, there is clear indication that not all communities are participating equally in the digital economy. Of increasing concern is the social polarization occurring among the haves and have-nots in access to and proficiency with technology. Recent data show that the gap between those with access to new technologies and training in those technologies and those without such access and training is widening and that the numbers follow economic and racial lines. Although this Digital Divide is alarming as the demographics of this country shift to a minority-majority concentration, the effects of unequal distribution of technologies and preparation for new technologies on K-12 education pose an immediate concern.

Many of the best economic opportunities in the digital economy are contingent upon individuals being computer literate, but often the educational experience for low-income and minority students is one that offers little access to technology, little training in technology, and few teachers adequately prepared to use technology in instruction. K-12 teachers who are underprepared in the effective use of technology in instruction cannot adequately prepare students for economic success and personal advancement in the new economy. With appropriate funding, careful planning, and effective training such as that associated with the Alliance+ program, however, community colleges are helping bridge the divide and enrich the lives of students least likely to participate and prosper in the new digital economy.

The Community College Role in Teacher Preparation

Community colleges offer a three-fold advantage for working with their local school systems to prepare teachers to use technology in instruction in meaningful and effective ways. First, community colleges are becoming the major point of entry into higher education for future K-12 teachers, enrolling nearly one-half of all undergraduates and more than one-third of all students taking science, math, and technology courses, and providing 40 percent of all teachers with their only science and math courses.

Second, like many community college students, K-12 teachers are juggling full-time jobs and family commitments. Time, distance, and transportation are obstacles to continuing education and professional development. The community college, with its rich history and experience in accommodating the complex schedules of working adults, is ideal for training and supporting busy teachers who seek to enhance their technology skills. Ninety percent of the population lives within a relatively short commute of a community college, and many of these colleges offer flexible formats and distance options to meet the variety of student needs.

Finally, providing occupational programs that establish and enhance careers is an essential function of community colleges. In this high demand and high skill marketplace, the typical community college is funded and charged to deliver technical training and workforce development as part of its community service mission. Providing current and future K-12 teachers with training in the effective use of technology to deliver instruction is one way community colleges can meet this responsibility. Another part of the typical community college's mission is the economic development of the area it serves. Making sure that students most likely to be left on the wrong side of the Digital Divide are provided opportunities to share in the possibilities the new economy promises is one way to achieve this objective.

These three advantages community colleges have for training teachers to use technology in teaching and learning emphasize the community college role in teacher preparation and in serving adult populations. In addition, community colleges have experience and a noted investment in the implementation of innovative strategies that directly support and serve minority and low-income populations. By training K-12 teachers to effectively use technology for meaningful learning experiences, community colleges meet students' technological literacy needs, preparing them to be successful citizens in the digital world. The Alliance+ model, a national teacher-training program, offers a strategy for ensuring that K-12 teachers are prepared to infuse technology into the teaching and learning experience.

Bridging the Divide: Alliance+

One focus of Alliance+ is to support teacher training and the integration of technology in lower income and disadvantaged K-12 school districts. Building on a number of recent national and local initiatives that help minority and low-income schools obtain hardware and software, Alliance+ aims to help schools determine how best to use technology obtained through these programs. Alliance+ resources and services focus on training teachers to integrate technology into the curriculum in innovative ways that enhance student learning and support higher levels of achievement. Alliance+ is helping bridge the Digital Divide by providing replicable models of K-12 professional development activities for teacher technology training in Cleveland, Miami, and Phoenix in school districts with high concentrations of poverty and academic need. Eighty-five percent of the students from the school districts participating in Alliance+ are members of a minority group, one student in five has limited English proficiency, and over two-thirds of the total student population live at or below the poverty level.

Alliance+ taps into the network of community colleges and their strong partnerships with K-12 schools to provide professional development and ongoing support to teachers in a computer-based world. Using a holistic approach to deliver technology-based learning to historically underserved populations, Alliance+ provides access, training courses, curriculum development, and teacher mentoring and support to help close the gap in the Digital Divide. The expected outcome of the project involves catalyzing higher levels of student achievement through the use of hardware and software. One assumption of training K-12 teachers in the instructional uses of technology is that they will create, develop, and assign computer-based learning experiences so that their students will be effective, comfortable users of technology.

K-12 teachers participating in Alliance+ are trained to integrate technology into the curriculum in innovative ways that enhance student learning and support higher levels of achievement. In Ohio, Florida, and Arizona, teachers work closely with faculty members from Cuyahoga Community College, Miami-Dade Community College, and Maricopa Community Colleges to upgrade their technology-based instructional skills. Drawing from more than ten years of successful experience helping teachers use technology in the classroom, Alliance+ employs four discrete approaches to provide teachers with professional development: (1) community college and K-12 school district partnerships, (2) a train-the-trainer outreach model, (3) a variety of supporting materials, and (4) continuous support. The *Savvy Cyber Teacher™* courses, central to the Alliance+ project, were developed by the Stevens Institute of Technology and focus on four strategies for incorporating technologies into a K-12 curriculum in meaningful ways:

- *Communications Tool*—using the Internet to communicate with experts or other classrooms from around the world
- *Real Time Data/Information*—accessing information that was previously only available to scientists
- *Publishing Students' Work*—publishing students' work on the Internet where anyone can see it
- *Unique Sources of Information*—finding information that is only available on the Internet

The Alliance+ model also features a three-stage train-the-trainer approach. Faculty from the community colleges participate in special institutes that prepare them to train mentor teachers from their corresponding local school districts. These mentor teachers, in turn, use Alliance+ resources to provide training for colleagues in their home schools. The three community college participants in the Alliance+ project—Cuyahoga Community College, the Maricopa Community College District, and the Miami-Dade Community College District—represent large urban areas with high minority populations, areas where the Digital Divide is likely to be at its widest. The work of these colleges and local schools districts illustrates how programs like Alliance+ can help narrow the gap.

Cleveland, Ohio

Among the 50 largest school districts in the country, Cleveland Municipal School District serves 74,380 students taught by 4,326 teachers in 131 schools. The student population is 70 percent African American, 8 percent Hispanic, and 2 percent other minorities. Almost two-thirds of Cleveland's children live below the poverty level and receive or qualify for welfare. Students with one or more disabilities account for 16 percent of the total student population. Achievement rates for Cleveland students are well below the state average—only 21 percent of the ninth graders passed the mathematics test, 49 percent passed the writing test, and 55 percent passed the reading test. When all required tests are considered, only 14 percent of Cleveland's ninth graders attained scores at or above grade level. The city's dropout rate of 19 percent is almost four times greater than the statewide rate of 5 percent. The neighboring public school district of East Cleveland City, another Alliance+ participant, serves 5,985 children, almost all of whom are African American. More than half of the families receive Aid to Dependent Children, and achievement rates are even lower than those for Cleveland. Only 4 percent of the ninth graders passed all required state tests. Training outreach for Ohio is projected to extend to a total 2,328 teachers by 2003.

Miami, Florida

Located in southeast Florida, Miami-Dade County is one of the fastest growing regions in the country, a factor that has presented a significant challenge to the district's 17,000 public school teachers. Children born outside the U. S. account for 23 percent of the student population, with as many as 350 new immigrant students enrolling in the district each week. More than 20 percent of all elementary school students have limited English proficiency, 58 percent speak a language other than English at home, and over 70 percent are eligible for free or reduced school lunches. With almost 350,000 students, Miami-Dade County Public Schools is the fourth largest school district in the country. The total student population is 52 percent Hispanic and 34 percent African American; 12 percent of all students are identified as having a learning disability by the time they enter middle school. Thirty-five percent of all eighth graders scored at or above grade level in reading; in mathematics, the pass rate was 45 percent. African Americans scored 38 percent lower than Whites on math tests and 34 percent lower on reading tests, while Hispanic students scored 18 percent lower than Whites on math and 19 percent lower on reading. At just under 9 percent, the dropout rate is nearly two-thirds higher than the statewide average. In addition to the Miami-Dade County Public Schools, Alliance+ training reaches teachers from the Archdiocese of Miami along with the Miami Country Day School. Almost 4,000 Miami-Dade County teachers are projected to participate in the project before its completion in 2003.

Phoenix, Arizona

Phoenix is among the three most rapidly growing cities in the nation and currently has 13 separate school districts within the inner city. These districts include 116 schools with 5,181 classroom teachers serving 114,760 students. The student population is 78 percent Hispanic, 8 percent African American, and 2 percent Native American and Asian. Limited English proficient students account for 40 percent of the total, while 82 percent are considered economically disadvantaged and qualify for the free or reduced lunch program. Despite a 95 percent promotion rate through the eighth grade, 48 percent of Phoenix's youth drop out of high school. Within the five years of the project, 2,500 teachers from the 13 Phoenix inner city school districts will directly participate in Alliance+ training. The Arizona Department of Education's Regional Technical Assistance Centers will provide training for another 5,000 teachers throughout Arizona. Through an online version of the training, an additional 500 teachers across the state will participate.

Conclusion

Alliance+ brings more than technology access to underserved communities. In its first two years, Alliance+ has trained almost 800 faculty leaders, developed over 80 hours of new computer-based curriculum, and reached over 60,000 students through technology-based learning strategies. The evidence on Alliance+ outcomes indicates that K-12 teachers are implementing a variety of technology- and Internet-based classroom activities as a result of the commitment from the participating community colleges. Because Cuyahoga Community College, Miami-Dade Community College, and Maricopa Community Colleges chose to answer the call, K-12 teachers in low-income and minority communities have been trained to create, develop, and assign computer-based learning exercises in Cleveland, Miami, and Phoenix. Even with little or no access to computers at home, students of trained teachers in these cities stand a much better chance of becoming adequately prepared to benefit from the opportunities provided by the digital economy.

Although the full impact of Alliance+ is yet to be determined, early evidence from the project indicates that as community colleges strengthen their relationships with school districts by providing technology-based instructional leadership, these partnerships are building bridges between adequately trained teachers and properly prepared students. Alliance+ connects the training of current and potential K-12 teachers with our nation's future workforce, and provides a replicable model of community colleges helping students cross the Digital Divide.

Note: For more information about Alliance+, contact Edward Leach, Vice President, Technology Programs, League for Innovation in the Community College, leach@league.org.

CHAPTER 9

A STRATEGY OF SCALE: FOUNDATIONS OF INFORMATION TECHNOLOGY LITERACY AND SUPPORT STRUCTURES TO BRIDGE THE DIGITAL DIVIDE

Maryann Fraboni and Susan Muha

The Digital Divide is a dilemma in communities across the county, as evidenced by the inadequate flow in the pipeline of qualified personnel for the new workforce. Carole Hoover, President and CEO of the Greater Cleveland Growth Association, underscores the challenge we face in the Cleveland area: "Corporations are experiencing enormous workforce demands, particularly in Information Technology, and reporting significant skill gaps among job candidates in regional applicant pools" (Hoover, 2000).

Cuyahoga Community College (CCC) has forged strong relationships with technology partners such as Cisco, Microsoft, SPSS, Oracle, and I-Generation that help us provide training to move qualified personnel into the new workforce pipeline. As we have developed these new training partnerships, we have recognized that technology training alone will not bridge the Digital Divide in our community. Technology training is the foundation, but at least two more important structural supports are required to build the bridge: (1) the packaging of IT skills with job-related soft skills and (2) the development of strategic partnerships between educational institutions and employers in the local business community.

Labor Market Demands and the Widening Ravine

The rapid rate of economic growth in northeast Ohio, brought about to a large extent by innovations in technology and new business development, has resulted in an extremely tight regional labor market where the demand for workers with adequate skills in various occupational clusters exceeds the supply of qualified workers. As a result, the regional economy is not operating at peak efficiency: employers are not maximizing profits, the growth of the region's tax base is impeded, and many individuals–especially those who are economically disadvantaged or underrepresented in the technological workforce–are not benefiting from existing high-wage job opportunities with career advancement.

Because the region's labor market relies heavily on both the service sector and advanced manufacturing, well-trained workers with Information Technology (IT) skills are vital to the region's future economic growth. According to the U.S. Department of Commerce, more than 50,000 IT jobs will be created in Ohio during the next 10 years. These concerns echo across more than 50 chief executive officers from the largest corporations in Northeast Ohio (*Cleveland Tomorrow*, 2000). The long-term economic vitality of the region is dependent on the collective effort of community partners who will drive strategic goals behind the vision of our business leaders.

Although some basic business and education partnerships have been developed, Northeast Ohio lacks a well-defined and tested system that includes all of the components necessary to prepare workers with the skills needed in key industry clusters that rely heavily on Information Technology. To address this challenge, Cuyahoga Community College has designed a partnership system and is piloting it as a model for workforce development. The model is predicated on building a strong foundation of authorized vendor and professional IT certification programs; however, the model's success is squarely dependent on the development of strategic partnerships within the local business community and the creation of a full description of successful employee performance.

The Training Foundation

Providing high-quality training for students to earn industry-recognized credentials was the initial goal in building the foundation of the college's workforce development model. We wanted to offer authorized vendor and professional certification programs that supply portable credentials, authorized training materials, and instructor certification to meet the needs of the business community.

Our strategy included the design of curriculum around vertical and horizontal skill ladders to target training for (a) large numbers of entry level workers needing basic training, (b) incumbent workers needing to upgrade skills to move beyond entry level skill attainment, (c) incumbent workers needing to upgrade skills to move to more sophisticated skill levels that require multiple certifications or advanced prerequisite skills and experience, and (d) diverse student populations from teenagers to the retired population.

During the past three years, CCC has earned recognition for offering the largest number of certification programs in Ohio, including authorized programs with Microsoft, Novell, CompTIA, Oracle, Prosoft, SPSS, iGeneration, Sun, IBM, Autodesk, and Cisco. These national technology partners allow us to provide affordable training and education to individuals who are not company sponsored. Offering such benefits as reduced curriculum costs, instructor training, marketing materials, technical assistance, and research and development products, these partnerships position CCC to deliver leading programs effectively.

Our training programs are populated by a solid base of options that spans multiple skill levels and provides certification needed by businesses for all segments of the workforce. However, IT skills alone do not necessarily indicate an individual's job readiness, and CCC's approach to bridging the Digital Divide is not solely about technical skill. The next significant component in our long-term solution has two facets: (1) developing the behavioral competencies that drive performance and (2) determining appropriate fit between the employee and the job that leads to productivity, satisfaction, and retention.

Beyond IT Skills Training

Many faculty can cite examples of extremely bright students who turned out to be poor performers on the job. Similarly, employees have encountered workers who are technically proficient but lack behavioral competencies such as customer service orientation, initiative, information seeking skills, and teamwork that are required to succeed a particular job. In preparing students for the IT workforce, CCC recognizes that technology is primarily a vehicle of transmission, and that the soft skills, or behavioral competencies, are necessary to enable students to use technology effectively in the workplace.

Through our performance engineering group, we offer employers the opportunity to determine both the technical and behavioral competency requirements for specific job positions. We use employee blueprints in a person-job fit framework to develop employee selection testing and interviewing, and gap analysis assessments in performance development programs and training needs analysis. Our person-job fit methods have been developed on the accumulation of over 30 years of research and are conducted by the industrial and organizational psychologists of our performance engineering group to ensure that the specific selection programs predict performance levels and are legally defensible.

To take our work one step further, we are able to determine an employer's corporate culture using our Culture Link™ survey. We use the person-job fit framework to help employers predict potential employee retention problems. The tool also helps the applicant select the best fit and acclimatize to new the work environment through a realistic job preview. This consulting work offers several advantages for employers and the college:

- Employee blueprints are fed back to the college to help refine or develop curriculum, thereby creating a pipeline of trained, job-ready workers for specific employers.
- Relationships between employers and graduates or other job seekers are facilitated by the various services of Career Place, which include an online job match program, job fairs, and specialized recruitment programs.
- Person-Job Fit assessments are processed in our computerized Assessment Center, on employer sites with paper-and-pencil tests, or with our portable computerized Assessment Center concept, giving applicants a quick turnaround of information in the hiring process.

Helping employers identify technical and behavioral competencies and cultural fit goes far beyond assistance with hiring and training practices. Our work falls within the larger systemic work that involves integrated business measurement and econometric modeling to discover the key drivers in a corporation's employee-customer-profit chain. This work, together with the years of specialized consulting experience, the contributions of our performance engineering group, and the services of

Career Place, has allowed us to connect people who otherwise might not have the chance to attain high-promise technology-related jobs.

The Strategic Partnership Model

As our work with businesses increased and we created job candidate feeder groups for employers, a new possibility for bridging the Digital Divide and contributing to workforce development became apparent. If we could strategically expand our scope of work with our existing client-employers into new and creative initiatives for workforce development, we could substantially increase positive outcomes. Specifically, we pursued the idea that giving more attention to the business issues of large employers would mean more opportunity to discover and leverage our joint capabilities. Together we could maximize our efforts toward workforce and economic development. The vision became one of a new collaboration for workforce and economic development that would engage our employer-clients, not simply by providing services to meet their needs, but by developing true strategic partnerships.

We intentionally termed this type of relationship a strategic partnership. The word strategic is derived from the Greek *strategos* for "general" and came to use largely in descriptions of military maneuvers. It was the general's responsibility to position the troops effectively before battle; strategy meant arranging battlements on the field for the best advantage, to make best use of each tactical encounter. The general rather than the foot soldier kept the big picture in mind. The general was responsible for thinking in terms of scale. We proposed to our employer-clients a strategy of scale involving collaborative effort in tactical moves for mutual benefit.

On March 14, 2000, after some months of demonstrating our capabilities, National City Corporation and Cuyahoga Community College signed an agreement of recognition and support that formalized a strategic partnership, "to share a vision, to share resources and experience, to share effort and goals for Workforce Development and Economic Growth."

Founded in 1845, National City Corporation (NYSE: NCC; www.national-city.com) is one of the largest financial services companies in the nation. NCC operates banks and other financial service subsidiaries providing client services that include commercial and retail banking, trust and investment services, item processing, mortgage services, and insurance. With $87 billion in assets and over 30,000 employees, its Midwest presence spans Ohio, Michigan, Pennsylvania, Indiana, Kentucky, and Illinois.

Our first, most comprehensive, strategic partnership to further technology literacy has expanded rapidly from the work preceding the official partnership signing and has touched every area of our college, involving dozens of our employees in a variety of shared initiatives. Across the two organizations, the number of employees involved, the number of interactions per day, and the number of different initiatives under way or being explored are evidence of the depth of this strategic collaborative. The design, development, and implementation of each initiative are shared by the organizations; each organization provides time and resources, and each shares planning and implementation.

In human resource consulting, our performance engineering group led the first initiative with National City by developing behavioral competency models for a number of positions within NCC's Support Services area of Corporate Operations and Information Services. Support Services is an internal help desk function, and our contribution to this initiative was to help National City create a world-class solutions center that would attract and retain superior performers while providing first-rate service to internal customers.

Cuyahoga's Performance Engineering consultants are working with NCC's Support Services to implement the use of the behavioral competency blueprints for hiring, training, and development. Plans are in place to replicate this pilot in other NCC departments, to develop distinctive competency blueprints for other positions, and, ultimately, to increase the pipeline of IT trained applicants coming to National City.

Cuyahoga has been invited to take on another key partnership role with NCC by providing *thought leadership* on issues of job readiness, culture acclimatization for new employees, person-job fit, professional development, and employee selection and retention. NCC has a three-to-six week, high-profile employee orientation program, the National City Institute, that provides new employees with a strong foothold in customer service, specific job skills, expectations for quality and integrity, employee policies, and the National City culture. The program involves coaches, mentors, and sponsors from the employees' specific hiring department and is designed to help new employees gain a sense of belonging, security, and opportunity at National City that will encourage employee satisfaction and retention.

Such deep involvement of the college in NCC's critical human resources initiatives dovetails with college training, recruiting, and placement initiatives. For example, Career Place, the college's career center, is building a collection of recruiting avenues for National City, and National City is offering the employee time to serve on the Career Place Advisory Board to guide recruiting, sponsor job fairs, and participate in the Monday Morning Speakers Series.

National City has made many contributions to our efforts in bridging skill gaps, volunteering to teach in our IT programs, designing new curriculum, and developing new training academies such as the Human Resources Professional Development Academy and the Professional Development Institute. Under the partnership umbrella, we have also become a preferred provider of computer training for National City's internal training needs. It is not surprising, with the shared focus on IT training needs and IT personnel, that we have embarked on two large initiatives that more directly address the Digital Divide.

First, *TechnoVenture*, an innovative computer certification prep-camp for youth, opened in the summer of 2000 to more than 400 young people. National City provided planning assistance and close to $90,000 to help launch the camp. Young people between the ages of 14 and 17 who wished to attend were assessed for placement in either the basic computer boot camp, the microcomputer maintenance with A+ Certification program, or the Certified Internet Webmaster program. National City provided scholarships for students from Warrensville School District, which has a large number of young people from economically disadvantaged backgrounds.

Second, *The Tech Prep–High Tech Academy* is a five-year joint venture involving the Cleveland Municipal School District; National City is providing $1,000,000 of the project cost. The Academy will increase the number of high school students in grades 10 through 12 in Tech-Prep, school-to-work initiatives, and college preparation. This academic program will help students develop skills in mathematics, sciences, technologies, and communication while preparing them for immediate employment, continuation of community college programs, or transfer to four-year colleges and universities. One component of the program will also focus on increasing teacher IT skills as a way of increasing computer training in regional schools. Through these efforts, local businesses will be provided with nearly 400 highly skilled workers annually for full- and part-time jobs, and students will accumulate college credit that can be applied in the workplace, used at a community college, or transferred to a four-year program.

National City Corporation is visibly committed to community reinvestment. In addition to these initiatives, Dave Daberko, chairman and CEO of National City Corporation, is leading Cuyahoga Community College's $20 million capital campaign this year with Jerry Sue Thornton, president of Cuyahoga Community College, and Morry Weiss, president and CEO of American Greetings.

Achievements of the strategic partnership between Cuyahoga and National City are measured quarterly for concrete advances within each initiative. A variety of measures are used, such as number of persons trained, managerial satisfaction with training quality, number of persons recruited through the college's Career Place, number of persons hired using the competency blueprints, performance and retention of those hired, number of youth receiving scholarships, and number of teachers trained. As we move forward, we will increase our measurement so we can examine the impact on IT literacy and workforce development variables and outcomes using structural equation modeling and other multivariate statistical procedures.

As the numbers of joint initiatives and employees involved increase, our growing challenge is to strengthen communication channels between organizational partners. To maintain the momentum that leads to accomplishment, we need to ensure that key people are informed about critical information at all times, that initiatives are tracked for detailed reporting, and that a single point of contact is assigned on both sides for each initiative. The overarching communication channel for all initiatives, and the partnership itself, was established early by designating a relationship manager on each side, persons who have enough influence in the organization to ensure active participation and who have the ability to strategize and foster the partnership.

With the flurry of current activity between our organizations, the tendency may be to lose sight of the need for the constant strategizing that defines the partnership and that determines our ultimate success in building bridges across the Digital Divide. While we may think we know better than to confuse activity with achievement, we know that we sometimes confuse the amount of work taking place with the strategic value of the work itself. We challenge ourselves to keep returning to the shared vision that gives us the overall framework to evaluate our work and to plan our next moves.

Summary

The foundation of any solution to the Digital Divide begins with IT training and exposing more people to training opportunities in their communities. Having established a curriculum that includes basic skills and a continuous development cycle to add certification programs, Cuyahoga Community College has put in place a set of essential structural supports for the workforce development bridge that leads to job placement and economic growth for all segments of our community. To strengthen this bridge, we need to continue our efforts in three key areas: (1) market-driven curriculum, (2) strategic partnerships with employers to leverage our resources and efforts, and (3) knowledge of the workplace in which our students will be expected to meet objectives requiring much more than IT savvy.

IT training is an academic advance toward bridging the Digital Divide. Like many community colleges, Cuyahoga, is deeply engaged in IT training activities. However, we increasingly have joined with local corporate partners to bundle this training with other support services that offer the workforce and economic strength needed to render the bridge solid.

REFERENCES

Cleveland Tomorrow. (2000, Fall). Cleveland Tomorrow: A Region at the Crossroads. Strategic Plan

Hoover, C. (2000, April). Performance Engineering. *Northern Ohio Live (20)* 8, insert.

CHAPTER 10

DIGITAL DIVIDE: A NEW TEAM FOR AN OLD PROBLEM

Robert E. Griffin

The Digital Divide is about more than connecting to the Internet, it's about connecting to opportunity in the new digital economy. Silicon Valley's Digital Divide is the gap between different communities in workforce, education, the economy, and technology.

–Joint Venture Silicon Valley, 1999

De Anza College is located in the heart of Silicon Valley where conversations and studies on the impact of the Digital Divide are as abundant as the number of technology companies. De Anza College is recognized as a lead educational institution in the area of technology training. In addition, De Anza is widely recognized for its leadership in multicultural education. Because of the two proficiencies, local business community leaders have invited us to be a partner in the discussions on developing solutions or interventions to address the Digital Divide.

Internally, De Anza College is addressing the Digital Divide through new formal support structures and through dialogues to define the issues. De Anza has defined itself as a learning institution. Our educational master plan articulates our belief that all students have the capacity to learn and lists strategies for improving student academic preparation and success. To this end, we are developing a Student Success Team that will include representation from all the constituency groups of our college (faculty, staff, students, and administration). The team is charged with responding to the needs of all students, but will initially focus its work on historically underrepresented students with below average math and English placement scores. Of particular concern is the relationship between technology literacy and student performance in math and English.

An initial discussion was facilitated by the author among a group of African-American faculty, staff, students, and administrators to help clarify Digital Divide issues at De Anza College. All participants shared definitions of the Digital Divide and gave recommendations on how to respond to the impact on African-American students at De Anza College, the first group of students to address in the college's Digital Divide dialogue. The comprehensive group included three administrators, three program directors, four faculty members, and five students.

To facilitate our conversation, the group defined the Digital Divide as a disparity in the use of computers and the Internet between historically underrepresented students and White students. We agreed that this definition implies that African Americans were not taking advantage of the digital opportunity to be gained from having a working familiarity of technology in Silicon Valley. We discussed barriers that inhibit particular African Americans in high tech careers and identified three key steps for De Anza College to take to address these barriers:

1. Dispel the myth that computers and the Internet are too high tech for African Americans.
2. Create partnerships between school districts, businesses, and community leaders.
3. Identify clear performance standards and learning outcomes.

The following sections capture the insights and recommendations that emerged from this initial exploration of Digital Divide effects on African Americans and other historically underrepresented groups, and what De Anza College is doing to answer this call to action.

African Americans' Place in the Technology Era

Members of the dialogue group shared the opinion that African Americans are not expected to be computer literate or have technical skills. As a group, we discussed the perception that some members of the business and educational community might silently agree that computers are too high tech or too fast paced for most African Americans. We agreed that some business and educational professionals seem to question the role and place of African Americans in this new technology era. Such an attitude is profoundly disturbing and undermines this country's claim to providing equal opportunity for everyone regardless of race, age, gender, and other diversity measures.

A sense among the group that the abundance of quantitative data that documents the difference between the use of computers and the Internet by African-American students and their White counterparts leads some to believe that African Americans have chosen not to use computers. The data show, for example, that African Americans are less likely to own a computer or access the Internet than their White counterparts:

	Whites	African Americans
Home Computers	44.2%	29%
Internet Access at Home	14.7%	9%

(Project 2000, Vanderbilt University, 1998)

We agreed that these numbers may be statistically correct, but without qualitative explanations, such data can serve to highlight the deficiency of some people and reinforce the competency of others. Quantitative data alone does not provide sufficient information to help get at the core of the problem: how to create equal or digital opportunity by race, gender, age, and economic status.

The group emphasized that we are committed to addressing the technology needs of all students and we must admit that our challenge for students is more complex than encouraging them to learn to operate or manipulate technology. It may be rooted in the same inequality that results in wage discrepancies, poor educational systems in African-American and other underserved communities, and other variables that have been labeled as discriminatory.

The challenge identified for De Anza College in changing the imbalance in academic and technological success among student groups is to reinforce the sense of worthiness, opportunity, and equality for all of our students. We must move from describing the challenges to designing interventions. We may even need to admit that the Digital Divide is an extension of the racial divide that has impeded the performance and progress of African Americans in business and education for a number of years. We must recognize and honestly believe in the capacity of all students to learn and grow when given the appropriate resources and support. Once we have honestly acknowledged the capacity of all students, we must begin to design institutional strategies to address the structural or organizational issues that cause deficiencies in our educational system and perpetuate the Digital Divide.

Creating Partnerships

The dialogue group suggested that the challenge of creating technological competence for all learners will take a collective effort by business, education, and community leaders. It will require that we shift our emphasis from assigning blame to that of developing plans that change the outcomes. These plans should reflect an interrelationship between education, business, and community leaders that demonstrates their understanding of the connection between academic and technological competency for historically underrepresented students. Members of the group agreed that it is not possible to fix the Digital Divide problem with a unilateral approach by education, business, or the community.

The group discussed several program options and types of partnerships that would address academic and computer literacy. One model the group felt would be particularly effective is based on a partnership structured to increase the academic and computer literacy of the historically underrepresented students and their parents, and to begin this work long before students come to college. The intent is to change the cycle of success for historically underrepresented students who attend De Anza College. The group recommends communication beginning with eighth graders and their parents. The parent component would provide a support base in the home and ensure that the parents are familiar with how technology could support their child's educational efforts. This partnership would also require that the community college and the junior high school, high school, and business community work as partners to support the student and parents. The ongoing success of this program requires that we maintain contact with the students and parents starting at the eighth grade and continuing through high school. Once students enter community college, the role of the business community would expand, with the intent of increasing the employment rate of historically underrepresented students in technology-related positions.

Chapter 10

Identify Clear Performance Standards and Learning Outcomes

The Digital Divide dialogue group concluded that even if, by magic, we could put computers into thousands of African-American homes, we would have no guarantee of an overall increase in computer literacy or use. Members of the group agreed that if we as a society value diversity and believe in the capacity of everyone to learn and benefit from technology, we must develop standards of performance and accountability for students and educational institutions. They discussed the difficulty of establishing performance standards and learning outcomes to address issues of the Digital Divide, but acknowledged that such efforts are already under way in certain college programs.

One such performance-based program at De Anza College recruits African-American and other historically underrepresented students as program participants. Through the program, each student is given a computer and an e-mail address. If students have no prior experience using a computer or are not familiar with e-mail, advisors counsel them into taking an entry-level computer course. While in the program, they are assigned a mentor and a tutor who work with them until they have an understanding of the role of computers in helping them achieve their educational or career goals at De Anza College. When students become computer literate and develop a trust in their own academic competency, they are assigned as mentors and tutors to new students in the program. Each student has clear performance standards and learning outcomes that are typically articulated as program goals for student success. Students in the program are expected to be successful. They are given the academic and personal support to help them get through difficult times and overcome obstacles.

For many historically underrepresented or first-generation college students, issues of cultural or community differences often become barriers to academic success. For example, the president of the college's Black Student Union admitted, "I don't use e-mail. I would much rather talk to my friends on the telephone so that I can hear how they sound." His attitude was not one of resistance to technology, but rather a cultural or social distinction regarding the use of technology. De Anza's student support program allows for cultural or community differences to be factored into the intervention prescribed for students. It is designed on the assumption that students can succeed, and it encourages them to take risks without questioning their academic competency if they do not succeed the first or second time.

The dialogue group raised the discussion to a higher level and challenged one another to explore the larger questions:

- What if De Anza College, as a whole, functioned like this program?
- What if we expected each student who came to us to be successful and had clear performance standards and learning outcomes for each student, regardless of gender, age, ethnicity, or economic status?
- What if we held students, faculty, staff, and administrators accountable for ensuring that students reach or surpass those standards?

Dialogue participants pointed to a number of De Anza College programs that enroll students who have no history of academic success, programs committed to helping students transfer, graduate, or achieve their career goals. In these programs, students are expected to succeed and are not given the right or permission to do otherwise. We discussed how we all have heard students explain that these programs gave them a sense of worth and ability to accomplish their goals. We had all heard stories of how, semester after semester, year after year, these programs provided a means for these students to survive or to change the pattern of their lives. We identified the common theme among these successful programs as trusting in students' abilities to succeed even when they were unsure about their own academic skills or tenacity. We ended our discussion with less a question than a call to action: What if the college was more like one of these programs?

Conclusion

Community college educators must make the necessary time and expend the intellectual energy to explore how the implications of the Digital Divide are affecting growing numbers of minority students. Community colleges have years of experience at successfully educating members of historically underrepresented groups; this experience can be translated into strategic steps to address the impact of this and other divides. The following recommendations outline seven strategic next steps for those who are interested in continuing the conversation on how community colleges might address the core problems or issues that are the gatekeepers for the Digital Divide.

1. Community colleges should assume that if students can operate a CD player, video game, cell phone, answering machine, VCR, and a beeper, they are technologically competent. Our task is to translate these technical competencies into strategies for improving their English and math proficiencies.
2. Community colleges should be proactive and assume the responsibility for developing partnerships to increase computer literacy of K-12 students. These institutions need to acknowledge the consequences of waiting for students to enter college without sufficient technical skills.
3. Community colleges should identify the best practices among their own programs and services and among those of other colleges that work with historically underrepresented students. These best practices should be shared throughout the college to assist in improving the academic performance of students.
4. Community colleges should promote the accomplishments of historically underrepresented students to help dispel the myth regarding their lack of interest or skills in technology.
5. Community colleges need to develop performance standards and learning outcomes for underrepresented students that duplicate or increase the academic success that is achieved by students in community college programs.
6. Community colleges need to ensure that sufficient quantitative and qualitative data are available to develop plans for improved student success.

7. Community colleges need to examine their organizational structures to identify institutional barriers or obstacles that deter success of historically underrepresented students.

We know enough to predict what the future will look like for our historically underrepresented students unless we change the outcomes of their educational and work experiences. It is important to examine the past and define the present, but we must act with our eyes toward the future. We must do more than build a bridge over the Digital Divide; we must fill it in. Filling it in will require that we tackle the tough issues of academic success and affirmative employment for all students. If we begin with these issues, we can fill the Digital Divide and create a new path for the success of all students served by our colleges.

CHAPTER 11

A SOLUTION FOR
DIGITALLY DISENFRANCHISED STUDENTS

Kimball B. Kendal, Patricia Grunder, Pat Smittle

Santa Fe Community College (SFCC) in Gainesville, Florida, is committed to providing quality educational experiences and student services to all students. SFCC, like most community colleges, has multiple missions: serving as the point of entry for disadvantaged students, supporting upper division college transfer, and providing career preparation, including the most sophisticated high-tech training for our local workforce. These roles are becoming increasingly difficult to juggle, especially as we are challenged to prepare all our students to keep pace with the rapid changes of technological advancements. One approach we have used is to integrate technology in all curricular offerings. Unfortunately this technology of integration, particularly the proliferation of online courses and online components in traditional courses, makes additional demands on students who already may have difficulty mastering basic reading, mathematical, and critical thinking skills. In our attempt to incorporate technology across the spectrum of our program areas, we may be exacerbating the disadvantage these students already face.

Recognizing that the Digital Divide is an obstruction to accessing postsecondary education and achieving academic and professional student goals, SFCC educators are working to increase technology access, improve technology literacy, and help learners build skills for adapting to change. For almost a decade, SFCC has been building action strategies to serve its growing numbers of digitally disenfranchised students by addressing three basic questions:

1. What programs and opportunities are we providing to ensure retention and success of these students?
2. Are we providing an active voice in communicating the resource disparity some students face because of this powerful medium?

3. How are we assisting students with their mastery of important skills that can ultimately improve their quality of life, their workforce experience, and their ability to be continuous learners?

The Challenge

In the early 1990s, the computer science program at SFCC was struggling with the challenge of general technology literacy and its associated retention effects, as well as the increasing chasm between technology haves and have-nots. At that time, it was clear that students without strong technology skills were at a distinct disadvantage in the classroom and the workplace. It was equally clear that the playing field for these students was far from level. Students who were completely unaccustomed to using computers, especially those without computers at home, were at a significant disadvantage in computer science classes. They were performing poorly, failing to complete courses, and failing to complete the requirements for their certificates or degrees at a much higher rate than we felt acceptable. During their examination of the program, the computer and information science (CIS) faculty identified poor access to technology as a major limitation, followed closely by lack of personal and academic support. CIS decided to develop a program aimed at increasing successful participation in information technology by the digital have-nots that became know as the Business Information Technology Career Assistance Program (BITCAP).

BITCAP was conceived in 1991 as a way to specifically address what have come to be known as Digital Divide issues. It officially began in 1992 as a Carl D. Perkins Section 132 Postsecondary and Adult Vocational Programs project under the direction of the CIS coordinator. Since it inception, BITCAP has successfully used the one-room schoolhouse approach to improve retention in computer programs and to move disadvantaged students into the information technology workplace.

The Program

BITCAP targets nontraditional students, minority students, and lower socio-economic status (SES) students. Each year the program enrolls approximately 18 students and helps prepare them for careers in business information technology. These students are served through a supplemental program designed to provide 24-hour access to computing technology, an intensive hands-on orientation to technology, ongoing mentoring and tutoring, and special activities to supplement regular courses and to promote cooperative learning by members of the group. In addition to developing fundamental technology skills, students learn to use technology to enhance their learning of basic language skills, business procedures, employability skills, and information processing skills. Upon successful completion of the program, BITCAP students are awarded a Data Processing Certificate. Most notably, the program has demonstrated more than a 90 percent completion rate.

Tests of Adult Basic Education (TABE) are used to assess the basic language and math skills of prospective BITCAP students. Students must be assessed at the 12.9 grade level based on the TABE composite score to enter the program. BITCAP students receive a strong academic and technical foundation through an intensive 33 credit-hour curriculum accompanied by mandatory mentoring and tutoring. The program, which takes four semesters and spans 16 months, supplies each student with tuition, books, and a personal computer. The computer is assigned to the student for the duration of the program and can be taken home. These computers are late model notebooks with ample hard-drive space, high-speed modems, and appropriate software. For specific program requirements, see the BITCAP Sequence of Study in Figure 11A.

Figure 11A. BITCAP Sequence of Study

BITCAP SEQUENCE OF STUDY

Course Number	Course Name	Credit Hours
CGS 100 MTB 1313 ENC 1200 CDA 1302	Introduction to College Computing* Data Processing Math Business Writing Microcomputer Architecture** *Prepare for:* ** MOUS–Word Proficient User Certification* *** A+ Certification* Tutoring classes–mandatory 3 hours per week	3 3 3 3
CGS 2564 CGS 1510 COP 1000 CGS 2540	Managing your PC Electronic Spreadsheets (Microsoft Excel) Introduction to Programming Database Management (Access) *Work study strongly encouraged* Tutoring classes–mandatory 3 hours per week	3 3 3 3
CEN 2503 CGS 2557 CGS 1580	Introduction to Networking Introduction to Internet Document Production Tutoring classes–mandatory 2 hours per week *Career Shadowing*	3 3 3
	TOTAL HOURS	**33**
	GOAL: Business Data Processing Certificate	

Access to the Internet is not provided by the program, but BITCAP students can get free Internet access from the locally operated Alachua Free-Net (AFN). The AFN provides free Internet access, free Web space, and free e-mail accounts to all residents of Alachua County. SFCC has been an active supporter of this nonprofit community organization since its inception. SFCC also provides all its students with e-mail.

For the first two semesters, BITCAP students are scheduled into their classes by the computer science program advisor, and they attend all of their classes and tutoring sessions as a cohort. This allows the program manager to monitor each student's progress and also fosters peer support and positive peer pressure to succeed. After completion of the second semester, the students must schedule their own classes, but they still receive assistance from the program advisor.

Hardware Support

We knew from the outset that access to technology was a major issue for these students, and the first discussions revolved around providing a computer lab for BITCAP use. The CIS coordinator was adamant that a computer lab would not serve these students because they generally lacked adequate transportation, had too many commitments, and had too little flexibility; they would not be able to get to a computer lab regardless of where the lab was built. Additionally, normal or even special lab hours would almost certainly not match the needs of this cohort. These students needed to have 24-hour access to technology, and the only feasible solution was to give each student a moderately powerful notebook computer.

Hardware is almost always the easiest problem to solve but, at the outset, this idea met with the most resistance. The idea of giving any type of computer to a group of disadvantaged students was seen by some at the college as wasteful and fraught with dangers, but to give them expensive notebook computers was simply unthinkable. All the stereotypical comments were offered: these students would not appreciate them; they would not take care of them; they were not capable of taking care of them; their homes were not conducive to proper care; the computers would be lost, broken, or perhaps even sold. The final comment was the most common complaint: "This is a waste of good taxpayer money." Against what at times seemed to be insurmountable odds, the program decided to provide notebook computers for the BITCAP students. In retrospect, everyone associated with BITCAP agrees that it has been a major contributor to the high success rate.

Disadvantaged students are generally not skilled at managing their time, have limited means of transportation, and have critical needs competing for their time. The notebook computers have given these students the tool to help them deal with these barriers by allowing them to work whenever and wherever time allows. The BITCAP computers have been replaced several times over the life of the program, but as with the other computers on campus, this was due only to the normal course of technology-mandated obsolescence. One of the more interesting statistics is that by all accounts the BITCAP equipment has experienced nothing more that the normal wear that would be expected of heavily used notebook computers. During the entire eight-year program, none of the computers have been lost, stolen, or destroyed.

Academic and Personal Support

In addition to 24x7 access to technology, the hallmarks of BITCAP are small student/teacher ratio, peer support, strong mentoring, and a great deal of personal contact and follow-up. The BITCAP program manager serves as mentor and tutor to all BITCAP students and serves as the classroom instructor for their first computer class, Introduction to College Computing.

Mentoring and Tutoring

The program manager, also known as the learning specialist, meets with all the students during the mandatory tutoring sessions and usually during other times as well. Because the students are kept in lock step during the first two semesters, the specialist can more effectively monitor the academic progress and the specific academic problems that students encounter. These sessions center on academics, but although tutoring is largely an academic activity, mentoring is a much broader and more nebulous endeavor.

Mentoring targets the students' general life skills. Many students have personal problems like budgeting, family relationships, child care, and transportation. Mentors help students learn to make sound judgments and decisions. In addition, students are assisted with job selection and, later, with job placement. The mentor shows the students how to match personality type with job requirements. BITCAP students are predominantly single mothers, so child care is a critical issue. The mentor helps students find reliable child care and often enlists caseworkers to find appropriate transportation to and from child care, work, and college.

Many single parents are trying to negotiate a very complex timetable of activity, so time management is a major area of concern. With the mentors' assistance, BITCAP students learn to set realistic goals with clear starting and stopping times for activities, to ensure adequate time for task completion by scheduling flexibility in work activities, to focus on the outcomes, to get most out of a day, and to prioritize tasks.

As part of the tutoring and mentoring activities, the program brings in guest lecturers from the college and community. Pertinent technology personnel are regular visitors: the director of SFCC's Information Technology Education department talks about careers in technology, various program coordinators talk about training and opportunities in their fields, and community employers come in to discuss their businesses. Other spokespersons include successfully employed former graduates, who enjoy a special level of credibility and who share stories about the struggles and rewards of the workplace. Guests from outside the technology fields include SFCC's former Coordinator of Fashion Marketing, who provides three days of topics on dressing for the business workplace, including how to select appropriate clothing and footwear, how to dress appropriately for the size and shape of your body, and how to prepare for a successful job interview. Often, representatives from cosmetics companies give demonstrations, hair and makeup tips, and ideas for selecting affordable products.

Although the guest speakers provide a valuable service, the primary purpose of the mentoring hour is to mitigate academic problems. The manager knows what homework has been assigned and knows how the students are progressing. Guest presentations are secondary to academics, and this fact serves as another incentive to academic progress since the students know that inadequate academic performance will result in cancellation of the guest lecturers.

Personal Success Factors

It is difficult to measure the increase in self-esteem and the positive transformation of the participants. Many BITCAP students enter the program with habits of failure that do not transfer into the workplace. Through high expectations for performance and personal responsibility, BITCAP helps students build habits of success. Acceptable workplace behavior is the guiding maxim. Employers want results, not excuses, so BITCAP tries to be compassionate without being excuse based. Students are expected to plan for foreseeable difficulties and to look for solutions. Students are taught that they cannot be successful if they are simply reactive; they learn to be proactive, to make arrangements prior to deadlines instead of excuses after the deadlines. Grade distribution is usually low the first semester, with a marked improvement the second semester as the program and training help students replace old habits with new ones.

Overall, students appreciate the opportunity that BITCAP affords them. For many, it is the first time they are treated as trustworthy adults and the first time they are treated with dignity. Because so many BITCAP students are single mothers reliant on public assistance, the program is not only bringing these students into the digital economy, it is also increasing opportunities for the next generation and helping to break the cycle of poverty.

Conclusion

An important limitation to BITCAP has been the required basic skills level necessary for program admission. Students who could benefit from the program often lack the requisite basic academic skills to attain the minimum admittance score. To meet this challenge, in 1999 SFCC instituted the Achievers program. Achievers need score only a 9.0 grade level or better in all areas of the TABE for admission. Three groups of fifteen Achiever students take eighty hours of noncredit coursework designed to give them experience with technology and to prepare them for employment. Upon successful completion of the one semester program, students enrolled as Achievers will be able to sit for the exam qualifying them as a proficient Microsoft Office User Specialist (MOUS).

A strong measure of BITCAP's success is the 90 percent completion rate, but equally powerful success measures may be found in the excellent academic records and personal testimonials of the graduates. After receiving their Business Data Processing Certificates, approximately 85 percent of the students complete an Associate of Science degree, and about half of these students volunteer to give back to the program by serving as mentors to the new class of BITCAP students. Their gratitude and loyalty are proof of the power of this program to change lives and introduce technology have-nots into the Digital Age.

Community colleges are under strong pressure from both state legislatures and the marketplace to prepare students to move smoothly and successfully into a high-tech world. Nevertheless, for every technology step forward that we take to serve our target population, we run the risk of further disenfranchising a major subgroup of this population and widening the Digital Divide. Programs like BITCAP can help ensure that we meet this challenge by providing digitally disenfranchised students a bridge of access, training, and support.

CHAPTER 12

INCREASING NUMBERS, INCREASING NEEDS: WHERE DO WE GO FROM HERE?

Gerardo E. de los Santos, Alfredo G. de los Santos Jr.,
Mark David Milliron

Underscored in Chapter Two, a comparison between the populations without home computers or Internet access and several key populations served by community colleges—those from the lower socioeconomic background, the recipients of GEDs, students from the center city and rural communities—reveals a huge overlap. That is, many of the students who enroll in community colleges fit the description of those who do not have easy access to the tools of the Digital Age.

A recent survey of community college students indicates that community colleges are providing opportunities either through noncredit or credit courses for them to learn skills they need in this era of information technology: "Among all credit respondents, 18 percent stated that developing computer skills was a major reason for taking classes" (Phillippe & Valiga, 2000, p. 3). The survey further showed that this was especially true for approximately one fourth of all first-generation student, single parents, and the unemployed.

Despite these opportunities, research indicates that the gap between those with access to computers or the Internet at home and those without such access is increasing. Community colleges must increase their efforts to reach more of our nation's have-nots more quickly in order to bridge this widening gap. This publication is a product of the first comprehensive international community college initiative to address issues of the Digital Divide. The ideas, research, model programs, and recommendations presented here represent the work of dozens of pioneering two-year college educators dedicated to the principles of democratic education and social reform. Longstanding programs such as Maricopa Community College's Ocotillo and Santa Fe Community College's BITCAP, as well as newer models like Cuyahoga Community College's Strategic Partnership, Humber College's Instructional Support Studio, Pima and Santa Fe Community

Colleges' short-cycle training models, and Tarrant County College's technology plan, offer ideas and models for community colleges striving to keep up with the growing Digital Divide in their own service areas.

Community college leaders grappling with the infrastructure, resources, programs, and services they need to help more students become technologically savvy may find it useful to approach the issue of the Digital Divide in terms of five separate but related parts: hardware and software, connectivity, professional development and training, continuous maintenance and updating, and technical support. This five-part framework defines the infrastructure and support needed to provide access and preparation for student success in the digital economy.

Hardware and Software

Community colleges need to have sufficient, current hardware and software to serve the needs of the faculty and staff. Beyond that, it is important, perhaps necessary, for students to have access to the hardware and software in libraries, resource centers, and open computer laboratories that are accessible on weekends and from early morning to late night. While open labs are crucial, community colleges also need other computer laboratories that are dedicated to specific programs or functions such as electronics or writing labs. The software needs to be appropriate, user friendly, and current.

Connectivity

In the simplest terms, connectivity allows all who have access to the technology to be able to communicate electronically, to have access to the Internet, to use this medium to access Web information from sources around the world, and to communicate with other teachers and learners anytime and anyplace. The college must be fully wired and should have access to broadband service through fiber optic networks that can move voice, data, and video.

Professional Development and Training

All the widgets, bits, and bytes and the best, fastest connectivity are useless if the faculty and staff do not know how to use them, so professional development and training are a must. Community colleges need to provide diverse opportunities for all employees to master the use of the technology through workshops, noncredit courses, credit courses, self-directed learning modules, and other options.

The need for training is constant. People who do not use certain aspects of the technology are likely to lose the skills. As the technology changes—and change is fast and constant—opportunities to continue to learn must be provided to all employees.

Of course, the most important target for development and training is the student. The options provided to the students should be rich and comprehensive, with noncredit and credit courses offered not only during the traditional times, but also on weekends, in the evenings, and asynchronously, using as many formats as possible (e.g., short-term courses, open entry-open exit, and the Internet).

Continuous Maintenance, Updating, and Replacement

Experience demonstrates that the equipment that serves as the basis for computer and telecommunication technology, while improving with each new model, needs to be maintained and kept in good repair. The more complex and sophisticated the systems, the more important maintenance and repair become.

Because of the dramatic pace of technology development, both hardware and software quickly become obsolete. If a community college makes an initial investment of $2,000 for one work station, for example, within three years an additional $500 to $750 will be needed to upgrade the work station so it can function effectively. Within five to six years of initial purchase, that work station will need to be replaced with a new, faster, more powerful one. At this point, further investments to upgrade the original are simply not cost effective. These factors lead community colleges to consider continuous investment, upgrading, and replacement issues when developing strategic and capital plans.

Technical Support

Related to the issue of maintenance is the technical support needed to keep both the hardware and the software in operation. Community colleges need a staff of technicians who respond quickly to faculty, staff, and students who have difficulty with the technology. Problems arise with hardware, connectivity, and software—the myriad big and little glitches that occur when people are learning to use technology—and the technical support team needs to be available to help users through these challenges.

Community colleges across the country use a number of approaches to providing this support, from a hotline that links the user with a help desk, to technicians who are available in large open computer laboratories. As more work stations are available, more people have access; as the technology ages, the issue of technical support becomes increasingly acute.

Guides Across the Digital Divide: Learner Relationship Management

In addition to the basic five-part framework, an emerging, more broad-based framework of strategies can be used by those striving to address the Digital Divide—Learner Relationship Management (LRM). In the metaphoric framework of building a bridge across the digital divide, this framework is analogous to us making more personal connections with students and, in essence, walking with them across the bridge. In this concluding section, we offer a brief look at LRM in hopes of catalyzing conversations about how a strategy such as this may help institutions in their Digital Divide efforts, in particular to focus multiple efforts toward the ends of empowering students.

As we at the League have worked with colleges facing technology-in-education challenges, including the Digital Divide, we often find responses accompanied by two regrettable tendencies: (1) unfocused and sometimes haphazard technology adoption, and, more disconcerting, (2) a disconnect between technology planning and the fundamental educational purposes of the college. As the bits and bytes buzz by and the righteous calls for bridging the Digital Divide continue, many faculty, staff, and administrators rightfully question whether, after three to five years of technology adoption, their technology infrastructures or their organizational strategies are heading in the right direction. The LRM framework attempts to address these questions.

Many institutions are making good use of rudiments of LRM, and a few are using the comprehensive model for bringing technology, students, and strategy together to improve learning. The institutions profiled in this book are good examples of applying such vision. Still, for colleges struggling to meet the challenges of the Digital Divide, workforce development, external competition, and increased student demands, the LRM concept may offer a road map to help maintain a central focus on their core business—learning.

From Lead to Loyalty

We all know how it works in the business world. We belong to frequent flyer programs with airlines, frequent lodger programs with hotels, even frequent shopper programs at the local grocery store. All of these programs have at their heart the goal of creating longstanding relationships with customers, moving us from prospective leads to loyal patrons. And while some programs are annoying or complicated, others really work. Many of us will take an extra leg on a flight, turn down a lower rate at a competing hotel, or drive ten miles further to deal with our preferred business. People justify these actions with comments about the quality, service, and personal attention that make it worth the extra effort.

The current version of this relationship-centered business strategy is called Customer Relationship Management (CRM), one of the hottest economic concepts today, with sales of CRM tools reaching almost $5 billion this year and expected to double by 2003. Although we are not fans of haphazard use of business metaphors in education or of tactics that reduce our students to drive-through consumers, CRM features some elements that are too powerful to ignore—elements that can help colleges ask hard questions and develop sound strategies for fulfilling their educational mission.

Foremost, CRM is focused on relationships. It asks an organization to look broadly at all its internal and external touch points and the purposes of the interactions in each touch point. The following chart illustrates a traditional company's matrix of touch points across functions (e.g., marketing, sales, and service) and infrastructures (e.g., Web, phone, and field).

Customer Relationship Management (CRM) Model

Proponents of CRM are quick to note that three years ago we had no expectations of tight integration across all these touch points, mainly because the Internet and its associated technologies had not matured enough. Today our expectations are different. Now when buying an airline ticket, we expect to be able to check fares and availability online, via a 1-800 number, or in person. Similarly, we expect to be able to purchase the ticket online, over the phone, or at the airport ticket counter. And we expect to get service (e.g., check our frequent flyer points or flight status) online, on the phone, or face-to-face. Further, we expect to proceed from one service representative to the next without having to reeducate each one and to get the *same* information from each source because our information is *in the system*.

Top CRM companies work to collect and use quality data about their customers to provide value that meets individual wants and needs. The goal is to let customers direct their interactions based on personal preference. For example, some people find buying a book on Amazon.com quick and easy. Others are drawn to their local Barnes and Noble to thumb through a book before buying. Still others integrate their experiences, browsing for cars online, calling to ask more questions, and buying in person at the local dealership. The trick is to provide a seamless, multimodal, technology-enhanced infrastructure that customers find valuable enough to use again and again.

From CRM to LRM

The logical extension of the CRM model to higher education leads to examination of traditional educational touch points with students. A college using the Learner Relationship Management model would ask key questions about how students are brought into the institution, how they learn, and how they receive services. Can students apply for admission online, ask questions about schedules over the phone, and apply for financial aid in person? Can they access an online syllabus, call for help from the tutoring center, and enjoy their in-class small group work all in the same semester? Can they check grades online, call a career counselor, or explore career options at the career center?

Learner Relationship Management (LRM) Model

These questions are more revealing than they may appear at first glance. Most of us would readily extol personal interactions as the most influential and constructive modes of connecting with students. But even these human connections may be poorly mediated by phone or e-mail, or degraded by faulty student records. An LRM approach calls us to expand our humanist proclivities by critically evaluating all the ways we touch students, thereby determining whether we are building productive or obstructive relationships.

Many community colleges encounter major challenges with even basic LRM applications. The information they provide on their websites doesn't match the information people receive over the phone or in person.

Student services are limited to one modality. Instructional options exist in either/or formats, offering students purely online or traditional classroom options, when students might prefer a hybrid. And a call to the college as a new or continuing student remains a labyrinthine experience, with callers forced through a maze of transfers and delays and misinformation.

Nevertheless, some community colleges have succeeded in engaging students across an array of touch points. Several have opened call centers with single 1-800 numbers for the entire institution. Others are rolling out 24x7 online tutoring support and using 1-800 "Beep a Tutor" programs for learners. Some are integrating phone and Internet technologies to enhance off-campus interaction for in-class courses, with language assignments submitted via voice mail and online threaded discussions held on key topics between classes. The measure of all of these good activities, however, is whether they serve as independent entrees or ingredients in a systemic recipe for student success.

Targeting the Outcomes

The argument might be advanced that this strategy is too technology focused, particularly for a cohort with little technology access. This argument, while important, misses the integrative capacity of this strategy to bring face-to-face, phone, and digital technology efforts into better alignment. Moreover, it misses the need to build an infrastructure that focuses on developing the student for a digital-driven world. Nonetheless, we must listen to the critique and ensure that a strategy such as LRM is clear about outcomes. If an integrated LRM strategy is to help bridge the digital divide, and if we are to avoid another business metaphor misapplied or technology budget misappropriated, then we must be clear.

Fundamentally, LRM strategies must aim at developing better relationship with learners to best meet their wants and needs. In the case of student wants, for instance, those with strong technology skills and good access may prefer to relate to us over the Web, others may feel more secure if they at least connect with a voice over the phone, and others may desperately desire face-to-face connections. Despite the boom in use of nontraditional touch points, it is interesting to note the College Board's recent study of adult learners, which reveals that if work, family, distance, or time barriers were removed, most adults would prefer to learn in person.

This finding also underscores the consideration that must be given to student needs. Clearly, many learners need alternate intake, learning, and service options because of their life situations. Other studies demonstrate that many community college students also may *need* a particular learning modality to succeed because of their lack of academic, technology, or social skills, despite *wants* to the contrary. For example, research suggests that if we enroll underprepared students in online classes without orientation or personal interaction, their likelihood of failure is high. But, if we start these students out with human-intensive in-person intake, learning experiences, and support services, and include the goal of helping them effectively utilize other touch points—to become more hardy learners—they can eventually develop the ability to learn well in multiple modalities. By focusing learning connections based on their needs, we enable these students to later engage other learning systems based on their wants. Put simply, through the effective use of LRM, we can foster the development of lifelong learners for the Digital Age.

The intersection of student wants, needs, and educational outcomes is the point where the *client* notion of education contrasts with the *customer* business model. If we develop our infrastructures thoughtfully in a client-based system, we can use our educational expertise to relate to our students better, help them balance learning wants and needs, and enable them to move toward becoming true lifelong learners. To work toward these ends, educators exploring LRM should ensure that as they strive to integrate touch points, develop hybrid models of intake, learning, and service, or create customized relationships, they target these strategies toward achieving at least four fundamental outcomes: (1) learners owning their responsibility for learning; (2) learners demonstrating content and competency mastery; (3) learners deepening their capacity to learn by using new modalities and strategies; and (4) learners forming a relationship with the institution so positive that the next time they have a learning need they immediately consider returning.

LRM and the Digital Divide Imperative

Make no mistake about it, community college students must learn well to live well in the Digital Age. To meet this imperative, community colleges must strategically equip and organize themselves to build powerful relationships with students that help those learners connect successfully to learning. Fortunately, today's workforce realities—those that make the Digital Age also the age of lifelong learning—give us more chances to touch students than we have ever had before. LRM can serve as a navigational guide for colleges striving to design all of their student touch points to best promote student engagement and learning. Ultimately, the thoughtful use of a strategy such as LRM can further the community college movement's longstanding commitment to be the catalyst of economic advancement, educational attainment, and empowering aspirations for all members of society.

Conclusion

Information technology is one of the drivers of the emerging economy, an economy that is global, highly competitive, and dependent on people as its most vital resource. To be a successful participant in the workforce, each person will need to have technology and change savvy. As increasing numbers of students enter through the open door with little or no previous access to computers, the Internet, or technology literacy skills, community college educators must take strategic and aggressive steps to provide the necessary access and skill sets.

Community colleges are one of the principal—if not the principal—providers of educational opportunities to the members of our society who have the least access to the information technology that drives our society and the global economy. The initial response of America's community colleges to bridging the Digital Divide has been positive. However, much more needs to be done. We invite all community colleges to be more proactive and more aggressive in dealing with this critical social issue.

REFERENCES

Phillippe, K. A., & Valiga, M. J. (2000). *Faces of the Future: A Portrait of America's Community College Students*. Washington, DC: American Association of Community Colleges.

AMADO M. PEÑA, JR.

I feel blessed having seen and touched the beautiful things that speak so proudly of who we are. Out gifts to the world are our history our art.

— Amado M. Peña, Jr.

Canyon de Chelley, Monument Valley, Spider Rock, Enchanted Mesa, Acoma, Black Mesa—these are names that evoke an aura of mystery and hint at birth of legends. These sites are part of an enduring, rugged landscape that speaks of the ancient heritage of a region now know as Arizona and New Mexico. This land, the people who live there, and their native crafts, are the threads in a rich cultural tapestry that is the inspiration for the works of Amado M. Peña, Jr. Using this trilogy of imagery, Peña studies the interrelation and integration of these entities, giving each equal importance. Peña, a mestizo of Mexican and Yaqui ancestry, celebrates the strength of a people who meet the harsh realities of life in an uncompromising land, and his work is a tribute to these Native Americans who survive by living in harmony with an adversarial, untamed environment.

Using bold color, form, and the dynamics of composition, Peña communicates his vision of a land, a people, and their art. He is a prolific artist with restless, creative energy that keeps him at work in his studios in Santa Fe, New Mexico, and Austin, Texas. A master printer, his serigraphs are noted for bold color schemes and strong graphic use of lines. His etchings convey quiet elegance in fine lines and soft color. The drama of his paintings is heightened by an intensity of hue and unexpected spatial relationships. Abstractions of the landscape merge with exaggerated human forms; blanket and pottery patterns further echo the shapes of the land.

Although his admirers come from different cultures and traditions, from all ages and parts of the world, the strength of his vision crosses such boundaries and speaks to them of hope, endurance, and the unconquerable dignity of man. These qualities that are etched into the faces of Amado M. Peña, Jr.'s art.

Peña Studio Gallery, the exclusive representative of Amado M. Peña, Jr., exhibits a full range of his original paintings, drawing, graphics, ceramics, and wearables. For further information, please contact Peña Studio Gallery in Santa Fe, New Mexico.

www.penagallery.com
1-888-220-PENA
penagallery@earthlink.net

THE LEAGUE'S DIGITAL DIVIDE PROJECT

The technological advances of the Digital Age provide unparalleled access to information. However, these advances have led to what many have called the "Digital Divide," where technological opportunities are disproportionately distant from minority and economically challenged populations. Community college educators must take an aggressive stance in finding quality ways to teach and reach our diverse student cohorts and communities. The Bridging the Digital Divide Project provides collaborative opportunities for community college educators, community leaders, and corporate partners to work together to better define this complex issue and build effective bridges to lessen the gap between the information haves and have-nots.

The purpose of the Bridging the Digital Divide Project is to inspire community college educators to take the strategic and aggressive steps to help provide the necessary information technology access and skill sets for a growing number of minorities and economically challenged populations.

During the 2000 Conference on Information Technology (CIT) in Anaheim, California, November 15–18, the League hosted the Digital Divide Summit in which Digital Divide leaders highlighted model programs and current trends and facilitated interactive focus groups aimed at helping the League define broad-scale Digital Divide projects. Speakers included George Boggs, President, American Association of Community Colleges; Norman Fortenberry, Director, Division of Undergraduate Education, National Science Foundation; and David Bolt, Executive Producer, PBS Digital Divide Series, Studio Miramar. As part of the League's existing contributions and commitment to helping address the complex challenges surrounding the Digital Divide, this book is Part One of a two-part series. This first publication focuses on broad, institutionwide recommendations and approaches to bridging the Digital Divide, while Part Two will focus on Digital Divide issues that community college educators, business partners, and community agency leaders collaboratively help to define through further League-coordinated focus groups, surveys, and information sharing.

The research recommendations, model programs, and successful strategies described in this book should provide useful background or stimulus for more complete conversations and explorations that we hope have started or will emerge soon in all academic communities. By moving beyond definition and dialogue to strategic action, community colleges are well positioned to help bridge the Digital Divide.

PUBLISHED WITH SUPPORT FROM ELEMENT K

Element K, formerly known as Ziff-Davis Education, has been providing complete faculty and staff training and development solutions to higher education since 1996. With over 900 information technology and business courses designed exclusively for the Web, Element K offers instructor-led online courses, self-paced tutorials, a comprehensive reference library and dynamic interaction with experts and peers. Elementk.com hosts an online learning environment integrated with a powerful administrative site for tracking and reporting, and offers a variety of libraries to choose from, including Office Professional, Computer Professional and Certification, Business and Management Skills, and Work Place Safety.

Success is determined by the ability to turn information into knowledge. Element K helps by enabling your faculty, staff and students to gain the knowledge they need to succeed.

www.elementk.com